Crazy Wisdom Tales
for Deadheads *

High Definition

---

* **Deadhead:** 1. An alternative place of mind that is open to both sublime and wild connections with the shamanic, sometimes, but not always, associated with the music and lyrics of the Grateful Dead. 2. An empty vessel for holding trickster and prankster spirits, inner shows that never end, and vibrational transmissions of Deadhead Enlightenment. 3. Any head curious enough to read this book.

Crazy Wisdom Tales for Deadheads

A SHAMANIC COMPANION TO THE GRATEFUL DEAD

BRADFORD KEENEY

STATION HILL ARTS
BARRYTOWN, LTD.

Published by Barrytown, Ltd., Barrytown, New York 12507 for Station Hill Arts, a project of the Institute for Publishing Arts, Inc., a not-for-profit tax-exempt organization in Barrytown, New York.

This limited first printing is offered in a trade edition and a special edition of 108 copies signed by the author.

Distributed by Consortium Book Sales & Distribution, Inc.
1045 Westgate Drive, Saint Paul, Minnesota 55114-1065.

Text and cover designed by Susan Quasha with Alison Wilkes and
    Vicki Hickman
Typeset by Alison Wilkes

Library of Congress Cataloging-in-Publication Data

Keeney, Bradford P.
        Crazy wisdom tales for deadheads : a shamanic companion
    to the grateful dead / by Bradford Keeney.
        p. cm.
        ISBN 1-886449-02-3
        1. Shamanism. 2. Awareness. I. Title.
BF1611.K32 1996
131–dc20   95-14788
                                                                    CIP

CONTENTS

Deadicated
to Jerry Garcia
& all the Living Dead
(especially Susan, George & Chuck)

A village without music
is a dead place.

AFRICAN PROVERB

A village with music
is a *Dead* place.

GRATEFUL PROVERB

Preface

Within and beyond the music, the lyrics, the concerts, the plugged-in happenings, the roses, the skulls, and the lightning, exists a shamanic wind that breathes imagination and life into all that is genuinely Dead.

This book is a mind altering instrument that helps create openings for entering into the Greater Head. For those not-yet-Dead, the following provides you with the necessary initiation.

But be forewarned: others have already discovered that this is a most dangerous read. These stories do more than muse. They penetrate into the deepest spaces of our most inner hungers, providing a movement that feeds soul into our heart-mind-body. Only enter as a way of leaving the familiar. Touch the shamanic mysteries that await all who desire them with unrestricted boundaries. Here lies the home of the Shamanic Dead.

It is no secret that the the band was blessed by the great Medicine Man, Rolling Thunder. In the same spirit, this book is dedicated to bringing forth the deepest shamanic center that connects the Grateful Dead to all the great and holy mysteries.

Awaken the companion sleeping in your hands.
When the Tales become connected to the Heads,
a great shamanic river will arise
and flood the earth with mirth.

Giving Birth to the Shamanic Companion

This book contains seeds that must be planted and cared for in order to be born as a shamanic companion to the Grateful Dead. Here you will find stories, recipes, and prescriptions that await your enactment, whether inside or outside dream time. You, your mind, and mindfulness must pour the water of Creative Imagination and Action in order to awaken these words into being a companion to the shamanic mysteries embodied by all grateful dead.

A Task

Lie down on the floor. Place this book on top of your solar plexus and spin it in a clockwise direction as if it were a record or compact disc. As your hand maintains the book's circular motion, imagine you are in the absolute center of a Grateful Dead Concert. This particular concert is the most amazing concert ever performed. As you pretend to hear the music, engage in the fantasy that the music is lifting you up above the whole crowd. Close your eyes and see yourself being carried into the sky by the energy of this sacred concert.

You travel across every continent on the planet and are finally brought down to a room where you find yourself lying on the floor. You open your eyes and find a book on your solar plexus. When you begin reading it, you find it presents a task that invites you to pretend that a Grateful Dead concert transformed itself into the book you are now holding.

For the next week practice this exercise. Lie down and create the concert that creates the book. In this way the book will begin becoming a companion, a shamanic companion to the Grateful Dead.

And Now a Tiny Story

Once upon a place, there was a devoted Deadhead who repeated the exercise given above. He did it once every 88 minutes throughout every day and night for 88 days.

One evening he found that his dreams were not that different from his waking moments. In his dreams he found he was also living with a collection of crazy wisdom tales for Deadheads. This book, however, had roots attached to it that came out of the earth. It was a plant book that grew a sentence with every dream.

Over time he wrote his own tales based on the sentences he saw in his dreams. As a gift to the earth, he buried the book you are reading in the middle of a great flower garden.

For the rest of his life he would take a daily walk in this garden and a magical thing would always take place without fail. Whenever he stopped to look at a single flower, he would hear a story or task spoken by a faint voice. Immediately he would run to his desk and write down what he had heard. In this way he became a gardener of great books.

A Tiny Task

Go visit a beautiful garden and take one pinch of dirt. Sprinkle this dirt over your *Crazy Wisdom Tales for Deadheads* and say out loud, "I hereby baptize my Shamanic Companion in the name of Mother Earth and all that provides a ground for becoming."

A Very Brief Story You Are Not to Read
*(If you accidentally read it, then immediately read the
following instructions as an antidote for the story you were not supposed to read.)*

There was a little kitten who told a little girl not to read the story you are now reading.

She read the story anyway.

The kitten then turned into the the girl and the girl turned into the kitten.

The girl, who was now a kitten, begged the kitten, who was now a little girl, to read the story she was not supposed to read.

The kitten and girl lived many lives going back and forth between becoming one another.

One day they forgot who they had originally been.

They never remembered.

They then forgot that they had forgotten. At that moment they turned into the words that became the story you are not supposed to read.

The Anecdotal Antidote

Write these words on a blue piece of paper: "I can not remember the difference between a fantasy reality and a reality fantasy." Carry this message strip with you for nine days. Take out your message strip many times throughout each day. Look at the words and say to yourself, "I can choose to be silent." Then turn over the message strip to the blank or silent side and say to yourself, "I can choose to speak." Do this as often as possible, reminding yourself that this is an antidote to the anecdote you were not supposed to read.

A Few Words Before Entering the Other Chapters

Know that everything in this book is connected to the relation-ship of the living with the dead. Practice being grateful for that connection. Here are the words for entering the other chapters. They are to be spoken every time you turn a page in this book. Turn the page to see these words of incantation:

I
am
opening

With the sound of one book hitting a head,
the light enters.
This marks the death of darkness,
enabling us to become grateful for the tales.

The Universe Is Made Up of Stories, Not Atoms

There is an old Irish story that is not true, but contains much truth. It concerns a librarian in Dublin who never went to sleep. Because this librarian could not sleep, he spent every evening in the library reading books. On the occasion of his ninety-ninth birthday, a seven year old girl asked him a question. She wanted to know what he had learned from reading all those books.

When he began to think about her question, a book about the Grateful Dead fell off a shelf and struck him on top of the head. The little girl giggled and asked, "Why didn't you learn to keep the books from falling on your head?" The old man knew there was some wisdom in the girl's remark, but before he could think further about it, the girl picked up the book and handed it to him. She immediately asked, "Is it more important to open or close a book?"

"What kind of question is that for a little girl to ask?" the old librarian asked himself. Within seconds he noticed that the girl was turning into a ball of white light. Within the light he heard her voice speak to him, "How do you expect to understand if you don't have a light to help you read?"

At that instant the old librarian sincerely believed he was facing the final moments of his life. The full weight of the situation fell upon him and he was suddenly faced with a life and death choice. The girl asked, "Will you use the light to help you understand what you've read or will you choose to become the light?"

He took one peak into the light and heard the wildest laughter of children and the ones they called "Deadheads." Their merriment began drowning his inner thoughts, doubts, questions, and uncertainties. He knew if he joined in with this laughter he would never turn away from the light. He would, in some completely unexplainable way, become part of the light. His life, as he had known it, would die and become one mere drop in an infinite ocean of illumination. The old librarian quickly turned away from looking at the light and opened the book that had previously fallen to the floor.

He lived another ninety-nine years and found himself unable to concentrate enough to read any book. The memory of looking at that light for one second distracted him from reading a single word. But for every moment he stared at a book he was unable to read, his understanding became deeper. In this way the light in his memory became brighter and brighter until it was no longer a memory, but a living light. That's how the librarian became enlightened.

From a sacred branch,
a guitar was carved into space.

Find the tree whose snake
ripples vibrations
through every living Dead.

Shamanic Trails of the Grateful Dead: The Great Center Snake

In the middle of the earth lives a black snake wrapped around a burning staff. Whenever this snake stretches or moves in any direction, the earth quakes. In this way we know and feel the power of the Great Center Snake. This same snake lies in the center of our own body and when awakened, tremors and quakes can be felt throughout one's being.

These things were told to me when I was a little boy visiting the most remote areas of northwestern India. An old man simply came up to me on an isolated dirt road and said this with no explanation. Afterwards he asked me to open my hands. Without any effort my hands opened by themselves. The old man placed a small twisted tree branch in my palms and said, "Jerry, this is the staff that someday will birth a musical instrument and connect your snake to the Great Center Snake. When the time is right, this will happen in its own way as it should."

He told me I should always keep the tree branch in a safe place and never forget what he taught me about the center of the earth. I started to ask him why he did this, but he left as quickly as he had come. I never saw the man again and never told anyone, including my parents, about what took place that day.

I grew up to become a guitarist and singer and traveled to many places throughout the world. I never forgot the old man and faithfully remembered his words and safely kept the twisted branch in an old leather box.

As a boy I did sometimes get out the branch and stare at it, wondering what it could do to me. It sort of looked like a snake, but it was clearly just a twisted tree branch. One day I fell into a kind of day dream and for an instant I thought the branch wiggled itself on the bed as if it were really a snake. It gave me a bit of a startle and I immediately put the branch back into its box.

That evening I had a dream the branch did turn into a snake. It crawled out of the box and began moving toward my bed. Slithering upon the bedspread, it eventually went right inside me through my belly button. I jumped and awakened to find my body shaking.

After that dream I didn't look at the branch for many years. Once during the early years of the band, some friends talked about the sacred life energy called "kundalini." Refering to it as the "serpent energy," they explained how it was a word and image originating from India. That was the first time in my adult life that the mystery of my childhood began moving toward some kind of understanding. I knew that the old Indian man's story about the earth's inner snake was related to this kundalini energy.

When I read some specialized books on the topic, I became completely confused. They provided very complicated explanations and ponderings on the nature of metaphysical realities. I found myself more lost about the branch than I had been when the old man first gave it to me.

It wasn't until I returned to India for a concert tour that the puzzle began coming together. It was my first time back to India since I had visited there as a child with my parents. I made arrangements to visit the northwestern part of the country and enthusiastically looked forward to what might turn up.

After the concert I traveled to the exact region where the old man had given me the branch. Along the way I stopped at various holy places and asked any willing spiritual teacher to help. Wherever I went, I observed the same picture on the wall. It was a picture of a man in holy robes. His palms were open and in his hands rested a twisted branch exactly like the one given to me. To my absolute amazement, the old man in the picture was the same person who had given me the branch.

I explained my story to every holy teacher who would listen. They all told me to keep looking. I was promised someone would be able to help me find the necessary truth. I cancelled my return flight home and spent an additional three months in India. I am grateful to say that I did find someone who was able to help.

On a late afternoon following a much needed nap in the countryside, I awakened to see the branch directly in front of my eyes. It was held by an extremely ancient person. He was well over one hundred years old. Smiling and showing few teeth, this ancient one spoke to me. "I hear you're looking for the snake." "Yes," I replied. I went on to say, "It's taken me most of my life to find you. What does it all mean?"

The ancient one took a deep breath and began speaking:

This branch is not for you. It is for all the readers of a book that will be written in the future. Other people from all over the world have been given a branch exactly like the one you hold in your hands. It happened to them like it happened to you. The Old Ones gave each of them a branch when they were children and told them about the Great Center Snake and how it can be connected to the snake inside your own being.

I am happy that every one of you successfully kept your sacred branch and returned to the place where the journey began. Each branch holds a story. You can't see it, but within the inside or belly of this branch a story is waiting to be released. The story of your journey is the story your branch has carried. When you allow yourself to write in the soil with the branch as a stylus, a story will write itself as if you had very little to do with it. Try this and see what I mean.

I complied and went to a large space of ground and began writing on its surface using the branch as an instrument for marking. To my amazement the story you are now reading, the same exact words, was written on the earth's skin that afternoon.

When I came to the part of the story you are now reading, the following words came forth. As you will see, they are written as a set of instructions for you, the reader of this book of crazy wisdom tales. The instructions now follow:

You, the reader, should take a piece of paper and draw the outline of a tree branch that is approximately twelve inches in length. Cut out this outline and carry the paper branch with you at all times. Some day you will find a tree branch that exactly fits the outline. This is the sacred branch waiting for you. When you find this branch, you will have moved closer to understanding how the Great Center Snake can be connected to the snake lying in the center of your being. You will have arrived at the same place of self-transformation as the musician in this story. The two of you will become one and the same in that both of you will be the custodian of a sacred branch holding a story. You will someday have to find a surface on the earth to enable your branch to bring forth the marking of its story.

When you find your branch, begin daydreaming about the story you will help write upon the earth's surface. Know that other people are also finding their branches and are beginning to dream about the story they will witness being carved into the earth.

You may now know that the original recipients of the sacred branches have been given different stories. Each story is a shamanic trail or level of understanding that provides a glimpse of the whole insight illuminating enlightenment. These trails lead to the Sacred Temple of Deadhead Enlightenment.

Enough has been said for now regarding the holy branch you are to find somewhere in the world. It is time for you to begin your journey toward the branch that will bring you to the center.

Before going on, it is important for you to know what happened to the musician who opened our story, who once upon a time happened to be me. He spent the rest of his life finding other people who had been given branches in their childhood. Each one had a story written on the earth for him to see. As he read each story, he began feeling more connected to the earth. This continued to happen and by the time he read the last story, he felt no difference between the earth and himself. He realized that both the earth and himself were made of stories.

The stories had been brought into the world by a branch from a tree. Each branch, originally rooted to the earth, had drawn upon the soil a story about how it is indistinguishable from the hand holding it and the earth receiving its markings.

The musician knew he hadn't written the stories. He had merely held the branch he understood was inseparable from the earth. In this moment of realization, he remembered the Great Center Snake. As he thought about how it quivered, shook, and quaked, he felt himself quivering, shaking, and quaking. He and the Great Center Snake were experienced as one.

When he went home he discovered a most beautiful blue(s) guitar. When he lifted it he could hear the rattling of a branch that had some-how entered its center. He was immediately flooded with the illumi-nating knowledge that his music and the voice of Mother Earth would forever be the same.

All of this took place because of a branch placed in the open hands of a young child. All that was needed to become enlightened had been freely given to him as a boy.

The musician never forgot the last lines of the story his branch wrote upon the earth. Somewhere on the planet these markings were cast:

Never forget to tell the future readers of this story that all they need to be enlightened is a small branch from a tree. When they find their branch, the snake within the center of their own being may become one with the Great Center of all that lives and is known through the holy mystery of story.

Prepare for the baptism into thunderous water.
Bathe in the symbol that opens the shamanic door
to the deepest forest of the grateful dead.
Do not utter the unspoken code of the hidden silence.

Thunder Medicine from the
Sacred Branch of Water

In December of 1945, at the same time the Gnostic Gospels were being discovered in Upper Egypt, a peasant farmer found a red clay jar buried in the white sands of New Mexico. Inside this nearly three- foot high vessel was a twisted tree branch with unknown markings on its surface. After forty-five years of research the code was broken and the branch's message deciphered. My sister, Carolyn, was present when the message was first uncovered, and she passed on this knowledge in hopes I would someday make it available to anyone interested in the subject.

On the tree branch was written the following message:

> This is the key to the next story. It is the next trail toward the Temple of Crazy Wisdom Deadhead Enlightenment. Find a tree that appreciates being the custodian of this branch and the next story will be revealed.
>
> Begin by contacting anyone who was on the second expedition to climb Mount Everest. Ask them about the stone found on top of the mountain. They will tell you about a symbol etched on the stone's surface.
>
> Make a drawing of this symbol and place it in the middle of your pillow. When this is done, wait for further instructions from a future dream.

After first reading this translation, I immediately contacted someone who knew one of the members of the second Everest climb. He knew exactly what I was talking about. At the top of Mount Everest the team had discovered a glass ball with a stone inside it. When they picked up the glass it shattered into microscopic pieces of dust, leaving only the stone. On the bottom of the stone was the symbol of a curve. Everyone was mystified by the discovery, but no one ever found out what it meant.

I followed the instructions given on the branch and made a drawing of the curve, placed it under my pillow, and waited for a dream. Months went by and I finally forgot about the drawing. One evening, after a day of listening to Ukranian folk music at a local festival, I fell asleep and had the dream promised by the branch.

In this dream, a tree appeared and spoke to me with a hollow sounding voice. It spoke as follows:

I am the tree that awaits the branch. You will find me in the forest closest to where you live. You will know me when you see me. Come bring the branch and bury it next to my roots. Then lie down with your head upon my base, hold a bass guitar over the center of your belly, and I'll talk to you in your sleep.

I told my sister Carolyn about the dream and she gently replied, "You're the first person who seriously responded to the message on the branch. Everyone else regarded it as an elaborate prank. Not wanting to be embarrassed, the whole project was abandoned and the branch thrown away. I had a strong feeling I should take the branch home and save it. Now I know why. It's been waiting for you. No one else believed in it enough to follow its instructions."

Carolyn went into her basement, pulled out a tightly wrapped box and, upon unwrapping it, handed me the sacred branch. I thanked her and promised I would tell her everything that happened.

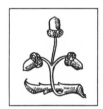

Off into the woods I went with the branch. For hours and hours I walked around looking for the right tree. I finally became overwhelmed with exhaustion and laid down on a comfortable place on the ground to have a rest. As I was nodding off I noticed a small sapling in the ground near my head. At that very moment I realized the tree had been found. It was a baby tree, a mere sapling in the ground. I had been looking up for the tree and I had to look down and even lie down to find it.

I immediately buried the branch, which was larger than the sapling, next to its roots and proceeded to take a nap. In my dreams, the sapling came and said, "Now you have learned that you will always get there no matter how hard you look in the wrong direction." The sapling explained how trees were the teachers of the forest. No one seeking enlightenment could proceed very far without some guidance from these forest teachers.

The sapling introduced herself as Evena. "I will teach you only one piece of understanding. The rest you must work out for yourself." Evena, the sapling, then showed me a large body of water with many rivers and streams flowing into it. "There is," she went on to say, "a branch of water that gives birth to twelve branches of understanding. You must find this branch of water and fill twelve bottles with its water. Take these bottles of water to your home and place them in a secret place. Tell no one except your sister about the sacred water."

I asked Evena how to find the branch. She said she could only give me a clue. I was told to take a vacation for two to four weeks and locate at least twenty-five different branches of water. They had to be found in a part of the country that truly inspired me as beautiful and mysterious.

After locating these branches of water, I had to select the five that emotionally and spiritually moved me the most. Each of those five branches of water had to be re-visited. While re-visiting each place I was to look for the shape of the mysterious curve I had seen on the back of the stone found on top of Mount Everest. The shape might be on the back of another stone, marked on the ground, etched on the bark of a tree, or even the pattern of the branch of water itself. Evena said I would know it when I saw it.

I took my vacation that year and went to twenty-five different state parks within a month. As hard as it may be to believe, I found the mysterious curve that had been originally marked on the Everest stone. I discovered it while wandering around the fiftieth stream. It was the last week of my vacation and the sun was brightly shining on the branch of water I was wading in. Losing my balance I fell and cut my hand on a sharp stone. I sat slightly dazed as I watched my own drops of blood dissolve into the stream.

That evening by a campfire, I was looking at the moon when I noticed that the cut on my hand was the exact same shape as the mysterious symbol from Mount Everest. I had found the right stream and had established blood relations with it.

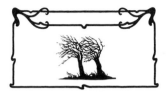

On the way home I went back to the sapling and told it everything that had happened. I went to sleep to see if a dream would come forth and it didn't. I then tried singing to that sapling and dancing around it, sincerely asking it for some guidance. The wind blew and I knew the sapling had heard my sincere plea. An inner voice sounding like that of the sapling told me to be extremely still and listen to the silent voice of guidance. I focused on my interior place of quiet and heard these words silently spoken:

> Tell the future readers of the guide that they must find a branch of water that brings forth their own inner voice of teaching. They may do this in several ways. The first path is extremely esoteric and the second path is simply esoteric. The first way requires locating Charles Henry's "curve of evolution." Charles Henry was a French mystic who rediscovered the harmonic mysteries of Pythagoras. The instructions for creating his curve may be found in the Appendix of the first book ever written by Jose Arguelles. Reconstruct this curve, place it under your pillow and await a dream for further instructions.
>
> The second way requires your drawing five different curves on a single piece of paper. Let your hand spontaneously create these different curves. After doing this, ask at least twenty-five people to guess which curve is "the mysterious curve of evolution." Give no further explanation other than they are supposed to guess without any knowledge as to what the curve is about. Select the curve that is chosen most frequently, draw it on a fresh piece of paper, and place it in your pillow. Await a dream for future instructions.

I can testify that these procedures work. If you sincerely follow these directions a dream will come. If the dream doesn't come easily, then feed your dream mind before you go to bed. Purchase some tobacco and place it on four quarters or pieces of silver. Place this tobacco and silver offering under your bed and regard it as a feeding of your dream mind. Continue this feeding until the dream is delivered.

When the dream arrives, it may be very specific or it may provide a hidden clue. What you want is some direction for how to find the sacred water of understanding. When you find this water, fill up twelve bottles with it. Keep these bottles in your home and tell no one about them. Know that you have brought a holy branch of water into your life. Think about this water every evening before you go to sleep.

I gave these same instructions to my sister, Carolyn, and she is now a regular visitor to the trees in the forest. She has found her own symbol of understanding and goes back and forth into the dream worlds where sacred waters of understanding baptize her into never ending initiations of mystery.

As for me, I became a custodian of the sacred vibrations that awaken all pools of holy water. I cannot speak of how my ability to create deep thunder with an electrified bass guitar is related to the bringing forth of inner rain. That topic is too sacred to be conveyed through dry words. It is enough to say that the thunder of my bass is capable of washing and germinating all sacred words residing within Deadhead beings.

Open the beat within your heart and see the
grateful eye that transforms dead vision.

Mickey's Heart & the Eye of Transformative Vision

When I was a child I took a long autumn walk around a lake near my uncle's cabin. During this journey I had an amazing experience that began with a sense of great calm coming over me. I subsequently looked up and saw a great white light revealing the wisdom of the cosmos. The experience was completely overwhelming, and it took many decades before I was able to talk to another person about what happened.

Years later as an adult, I asked a professional hypnotist to regress me back to my childhood with the hope that I would be able to re-experience the vision. The hypnotist, Mr. Roland, was perfect for the job. He put me into trance and I began reliving the afternoon in which the mysterious experience took place. However, when it came time to see the vision of light, my inner screen of viewing went blank and the following words were heard:

> Your vision was seen through your heart. Your heart is the instrument
> for divine perception.

Something particularly strange had taken place before I saw the hypnotist. When I arrived at his office, I was surprised to discover I had come forty-five minutes too early. I had never before misjudged time by such a magnitude and was startled by the miscalculation. Since a bookstore was nearby, I proceeded to browse through their collection and came across an extremely rare book. It was an esoteric text about the Sufi mystic, Ibn 'Arabi, who lived between 1165 and 1240. I purchased it and didn't open it for examination until after my bout with the hypnotist.

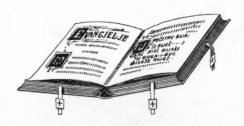

On the way home from the hypnotist's office, I couldn't stop thinking about how strange it was not to be able to see the vision of light
under hypnosis. I kept hearing the words that had been spoken to me:
*Your vision was seen through your heart. Your heart is the instrument for
divine perception.* Perhaps I was unconsciously afraid to relive the great
vision, afraid it would swallow up my rational life as I now knew it. If
this were the case, it would explain my nervous mistake of showing up
too early for the appointment.

When I arrived home I examined the rare book about Ibn 'Arabi. The
first thing I read when I opened it was about how the heart is a subtle
organ enabling one to perceive the Form of God. It was described as
the mystic's eye that sees the holy light. Although this "heart" is related
to the organ of flesh located on the left side of the body, it is a spiritual
organ, the central organ of our mystical physiology. These mystical or-
gans, sometimes called "chakras" in India, help carry and transform
the mystical energy called "kundalini."

The great Sufi mystic, Ibn 'Arabi, understood the nature and opera-
tion of the heart as an eye of transformative vision. When the heart is
awakened by one's pure intention to participate in creation, mystical
doors of experience are opened. The mystic then becomes a body, a
medium, through which the divine expresses and manifests its acts of
creation. The heart is the door connecting us with the divine spirit's
breath of creative expression.

I soon realized that my visit to the hypnotist had less to do with re-
experiencing my childhood vision than with confirming the truth of
the mystical heart. The words of Ibn 'Arabi fell into my mind as I tried
to face my early mystical vision, and his words fell into my hands
with the rare book found due to miscalculating the hypnotist's appointment. The book I found was not a new book. It had been owned

by someone else because there were very tiny scribblings made throughout the margins. I couldn't make sense of the scribblings, but one day I had the idea to examine them under magnification using a stereoscope. When seen through new lenses, what appeared was a microscopic text. Someone had written another book in print too small to be seen by the unaided eye.

The secret text began with these words:

> *I am the holder of the branch which carries this story.* Over the centuries the secret recipes of Ibn 'Arabi have been preserved in this sacred tree branch. It was passed from one generation of mystics to another. When the appropriate time arrives for mass cultural transformation, the mystical recipes will be released to the Deadheads. These recipes are prescriptions for action. If a person sincerely follows them, they will assist in the opening of one's mystical heart, the door to the other worlds. In this way the Dead will help raise the Embalmed Living.
>
> What follows are the mystical recipes carefully preserved and saved for this moment in human history. They are not intended to be understood. They are not for the mind of reason. That mind has not minded the laws of the heart. These recipes are for lubricating the hinges of the mystical door of the heart. They are to be exercised rather than understood.
>
> Do not talk about any recipe unless you have first performed it.

The Three Mystical Recipes of Ibn 'Arabi

RECIPE ONE
Preparing Your Heart

Ask another person to help you draw an outline of your whole body. You probably will have to tape pieces of paper or newspaper together to create a large enough paper sheet to contain yourself. When this is done draw your heart on the outline with the color you find most sacred and indicative of mystery. Inside this heart, use a pencil to write down the name of everything you desire in life. If you run out of room within the space of your heart, then write on top of what you previously have written.

Go to the library and gather as many names of mystics as you can find. These mystics may be from any culture and era of history. With a black marking pen write the names of these mystics over what was written as your desires. When this is done, use an eraser to remove all the previous pencil writing. Your heart will now contain the freed space of your former desires with many mystics on guard.

With a lit white candle, allow wax to drip over the entire surface of the heart within your body outline. The whole heart should be covered with a thick layer of white candle wax.

Cut one piece of your hair and lay it upon this bed of wax. With a lit red candle, allow the red wax to cover this piece of hair. This is done to remind you of the link between you and your outline.

Select the book you believe is the holiest book in the world. Open it up at random and point your finger to a sentence. Write the sentence down. Repeat this procedure five times. Examine your five sacred sentences and choose the one that most deeply speaks to you. Write this sacred sentence on a tiny piece of white paper. Make certain you write it as tiny as you possibly can.

Fold this tiny piece of paper and attach it with tape to the "non-head" side of a silver coin. A quarter will work fine. Place this coin into the center of your heart with the sacred sentence face down. This will be the sacred heart of your heart. Using another white candle, allow wax to fully cover this heart and make it one with the previously melted wax.

With the sacred branch you previously found, press it into the center of the sacred heart, making a marked impression upon the wax covering it. Within that impression, use a needle to etch the symbol of the mysterious curve you earlier created or found.

Place this outline of yourself underneath your bed so its heart lines up with your biological heart. Purchase a small flashlight and place it next to the heart underneath your bed. When you go to sleep in the evening, turn on the flashlight making certain it illuminates the sacred heart. Go to sleep thinking about the illumined heart underneath your physical body. When you have a dream about your sacred heart, proceed to the next recipe.

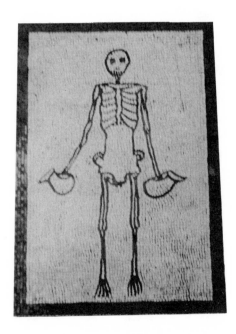

RECIPE TWO
Capturing the Light

After you dream your sacred heart, remove the flashlight illuminating the heart underneath your bed. Take out its light bulb and trace it on a small piece of paper.

Take a photograph of the heart underneath your bed. When the picture is developed, make a xerox copy of it. Copy it again, but reduce it's size. Keep reducing it over and over again until you only have a small dot that will fit within the tracing of your light bulb. (If a copy becomes too faint, trace its outline with a dark pen so it may be xeroxed and reduced to the appropriate size.) Glue the dot inside the light bulb's outline.

With a bandage attach this heart within a light over the left side of your chest so it will be above your own biological heart. Wear this for three days. At the end of that time remove the heart within the light and sprinkle it with water from a stream or branch you believe is beautiful and special. This water may be the water you found in the previous story.

Go to the nearest state park and find a tree that appears wise to you. Ask the tree for permission to remove a branch from it. Carefully remove a tiny branch and take it home with you. Using white thread, attach the heart within a light to this branch and place it over the heart underneath your bed.

Before you go to sleep make up a dream about the branch and write this fictitional dream on a piece of paper. Place the dream underneath your bed, between the two hearts. Wait until something mysterious happens to you in your dreams. You will know it when it happens. When it does, you may proceed to the final recipe.

RECIPE THREE
Creating a Story About Your Illumined Heart

Remove the sacred branch with a heart from underneath your bed. Attach a sharpened pencil to it enabling you to use it as a writing instrument. On the night of a full moon, wait until midnight to do this task. Fill a room with twenty-five lit candles. Bring your body outline into the center area of this room and turn it over. Using the branch pencil write a story on the backside of this outline. The story is to be created by your imagination in the following way.

Write down the three most important words or metaphors that relate to the dreams you had from recipes one and two. The story must be written so as to include these three metaphors. The story should be short, mysterious, and sacred. When you complete the story, roll up the outline around the branch. Tie up this story roll with three pieces of white string, wrap the entire roll with aluminum foil, and bury it in your backyard or in a local field.

Place one candle in the ground over the spot where you buried the story roll. Light the candle for no more than three minutes whenever there is a full moon. When the candle is half way used, dig up the story roll and unpack it. Read the story outloud to yourself. Wrap it up again, bury it in the same place, set up a new candle, and repeat the procedure. Do this a total of three times.

After the third candle has been used, burn the story roll and place the ashes into a tiny jar. Using your sacred branch mark each of the three candles with the initials, "I. A." Carry them into every room in your home and work place. Allow at least one drop of wax to become part of each of these rooms. Into each drop of wax place a pinch of the ashes. Practice appreciating how the story of your sacred heart is now a part of every room in your life.

I gave this story about the mystical recipes of Ibn ʿArabi to my hypnotist and explained how the recipes were designed to help one open the mystical door of one's own heart of transformative vision. He proceeded to exercise them with the singular purpose and intention to perceive mystery. He also vowed to never talk to anyone about these recipes unless they, too, were actually practicing them.

The hypnotist developed a completely new way of talking to people's mystical hearts. He stopped calling himself a hypnotist and became known as a storyteller, creating individualized tales that help people transform personal obstacles into mythological episodes within their life story.

After making many stories with numerous clients, he retired and went to live in the woods. I received a letter saying he was still learning from the trees and streams. He hoped he would learn enough to be accepted as a student of the grasshoppers and turtles. The last communication I received expressed his mysterious promise to send a branch that needed to be attached to the back of a turtle's shell. He also requested passing on the following words to the readers of this story, the heart tale. I faithfully pass on his words to you:

> *You have now come to the end of the heart story. I'll let you know I'm still around when you discover my teacher, the great turtle who carries an important branch. The beat of that turtle's mystical heart will be awakened by sacred sticks that find their way to the heart of your drum.*

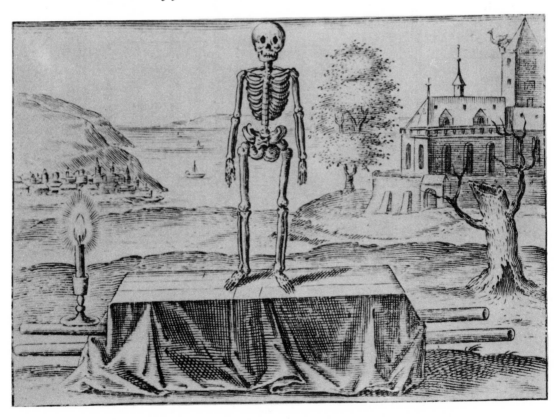

There was once a merry berry
that swallowed itself
and began choking on its own laughter.
It was saved by a prank
that eliminated the crank
that threatened to pick off the merry
from that berry.

Merry Pranks

This story is not really a story. It's a set of instructions for you to perform some merry pranks and weird conduct in the world. When you do these weird things, you will encounter the enactment of a story about yourself practicing weirdness. In other words, you are invited to become the author and performer of this story. It is a drama to be lived and experienced by following these instructions.

One

Purchase twelve copies of *Crazy Wisdom Tales for Deadheads*. Give a copy to twelve people you know. You must believe each person has a chance of becoming enlightened in this lifetime. Ask each person to do you a favor and read the book. Ask them to choose the most enlightening sentence and the most unenlightening sentence in the book. This will result in your collecting twelve enlightening sentences and twelve unenlightening sentences.

Rank order each list of statements from most enlightening to least enlightening. For each statement, create a statement that is its opposite. Place these opposite statements in an envelope and write this quotation on the outside of the envelope:

A great truth is a truth whose opposite is also a great truth.
— *Niels Bohr*

Give these packages of opposite truths back to the twelve people who helped you and thank them for their participation in helping you find enlightenment.

Two

The following week, mail an empty letter to the twelve people who participated in your last task. With a second letter ask them to suggest someone they believe is open to receiving the kind of truth this book helps bring forth.

Mail each of these people an envelope with this quotation inside it:

Nothing is more real than nothing.
— *Samuel Beckett*

Wait a week and then send each person an empty box.

Wait another week and send them this message in the mail:

Your friend read *Crazy Wisdom Tales for Deadheads* and caused me to send you the reality of nothing.

Three

Write an anonymous letter telling the story of what you did in the two previous weird tasks. Make twelve copies of this letter and leave it inside twelve popular magazines or newspapers in a public library.

Sit in a place where you can observe a person finding your anonymous letter. Write down everything you see about this person, how they are dressed, their body movements, the color of their hair and eyes, and so forth.

Write an anonymous letter about how this person's life changed due to finding the previous letter in the library. Make twelve copies of this letter and mail it to twelve psychotherapists. Do not leave your name or address, but sign it, "An Agent of Deadhead Enlightenment."

Four

On a single sheet of paper draw the outline of a sacred tree branch with a heart in its center. Underneath this branch write these words:

Many of us are moving toward Deadhead Enlightenment. We join you in the journey of this great and ridiculous purpose.

Go to a library or bookstore that has a copy of *Crazy Wisdom Tales for Deadheads* and place this paper on the page number you are now reading. If the library does not have the book, get them to order it. If they refuse, donate a copy, leaving your paper branch inside.

Five

On the side of a piece of paper write the word, ENLIGHTENMENT.
On the opposite side of the paper write, IGNORANCE.
On another piece of paper write,
THE OPPOSITE OF A TRUTH IS AN EVEN GREATER TRUTH.
On the backside of this paper write,
THE REVERSE SIDE ALSO HAS A REVERSE SIDE.
Fold the first piece of paper and then tape it onto the center of the second piece.
Make twelve of these doubled messages and place them into the world.

Six

Take a piece of paper and cut out a three inch circle in its center. Around the circumference of this circular hole write the words,
NOTHING REVEALS REALITY.
In a public place look through the hole of this paper as if you were experiencing another world. When someone asks what you are doing, hand them the paper and say, "The operating instructions are revealed on the instrument."

For More Merry Pranks
see page 88

The Fool

And the Great Spirit commanded you
to build a great ark.
And so you will.
This is how the Dead find a field that preserves the
dancing of dream.

Building an Ark

Yesterday I met someone who had gone to a bookstore, opened a book, and found a message in it. On the back cover of the book were these words,

> Since you have opened the book and found this ticket, consider your-self initiated into the beginning of a mysterious Deadhead adventure. You are now admitted and may proceed to the public library in the town center.

He immediately went to the library and sat down at a table. Having no idea what he was supposed to do, he just continued sitting there without a book. At the same exact time, I was sitting at the same table in the library writing a story. I had written the first two paragraphs and was stuck. I didn't know what to write next. I put down my pencil and introduced myself to the gentleman sitting across from me.

He began telling me what had happened to him. I immediately began to feel the rush of a great mystery being born. Interrupting him, I said, "Here, look at the story I'm trying to write." When he read the first two paragraphs, he read what you have read so far. As hard as this is to believe, I had written about what had happened to him.

"What do we do now?" the man asked. I replied, "Perhaps we should look around the library and see if there are any clues. Didn't the story begin when you opened a book?" I asked him what the book was about and he said it was on the literary contributions of the mystical poet, Rumi. We immediately went to the library's card catalogue and looked up every book on Rumi we could find and began browsing through them.

After several hours of exploring these books, the man I now called Chuck, said, "Look at this. It's the next clue." He handed me a book with some words underlined in it. The words, written by Rumi, had a handwritten message next to them saying, "The second clue." The clue was this quotation of Rumi:

> *Start a huge, foolish project*
> *like Noah.*
> *It makes absolutely no difference*
> *what people think of you.*

Chuck and I knew we were being told by some mysterious process to go start a "huge, foolish project." We discussed what we could possibly do together and found neither of us had any carpentry skills. That ruled out building a nautical ark. We soon ran out of time and promised to give one another a phone call that evening to decide what to do next.

When I went home I found a purple colored envelope underneath my door. On the inside was a purple piece of paper with this quotation:

> **To see truth, contemplate all phenomena as a lie.**
>
> — Thaganapa

I immediately called Chuck and discovered he, too, had received a purple letter. His quotation was related to the one I had received:

> **All great truths begin as blasphemies.**
>
> — George Bernard Shaw

We knew these were new clues to help us figure out our huge, foolish project. We agreed to return to the library the next day and conduct some more research on the great spiritual poet, Rumi.

When we arrived at the library we were surprised to find all the books on Rumi had disappeared. On the shelf where they should have been was a purple envelope with this poem written by Rumi:

> Out beyond ideas of wrongdoing and rightdoing,
> there is a field. I'll meet you there.
>
> When the soul lies down in that grass,
> the world is too full to talk about.
>
> Ideas, language, even the phrase 'each other'
> don't make sense.

After reading the poem, Chuck and I left the library and drove to an open field. We were silly and laughed the entire time like children playing after school. We ran in circles throughout the open field and skipped for the first time in several decades. It felt like a dance and brought back all the pure perceptions we used to have as children.

At one point I looked at Chuck and saw him fall to the ground with exhaustion. He shouted out, "I am going to say something important. I will only say it once and it will come out of my mouth without any interference from my educated mind. I'm too tired to think and given what has happened to us, I don't believe anything is rational anymore." He then spoke the following speech and not a word has been forgotten:

"I have nothing to say or write that is meant to impress an audience. I do not want to turn others into my customers. This cheapens my words and vulgarizes their participation in the greater community of creative beings. If I appear to have an answer, or appear to be wise, then I have deceived everyone. I must only speak to my gods, the ones who know me as a child. They are happy when they see us chasing

one another in an open field. They are pleased when we are silly and funny. It is they who want us to build a huge and foolish project."

Chuck's words freed me to stand up and shout out:

"I, too, can speak without a mind that cares to judge and interpret. To provide bait for popularity is to lose one's happy soul. I want the gods to laugh with us and turn our amusements into musings for the field. It is time to build a most foolish project."

Since it was beginning to get dark, we decided to return to our homes. On the way to the car Chuck said, "Let's take something from the field to remind us of our time together." He said this as we walked beneath a huge maple tree. We heard a cackling sound, looked up and saw a branch falling from the tree. We jumped out of the way and the branch landed in front of our feet. Chuck picked up the branch, broke it in two and said, "This is the branch that will remind us of entering the field of children's dreams." I teased him about becoming a poet and he replied, "That's it! Let's build a book. I don't know what kind of book, but let's talk about it next week." Since he had to go out of town on some business, we arranged to meet at the field the following week.

During the time we were waiting, each of us had a dream unlike any dream we had ever had before. Chuck found himself dreaming of a great desert of sand. In the middle of this desert, he found a great stone monolith with these words etched into it:

Out of Time

Once upon a time, time wasn't a four letter word. Time was not known, either by broken or unbroken line. Only possibility breathed through a distant wind.

A hand clapped, opening a shower of sand. Falling upon a silent tent, an occupant was awakened.

A birth distinguished what had been from what was no more.

Possibility came into the flesh. After the fall, human beings began to reach and hold. Bodies contorted into rhythms of loss and expectation. Lines of desire became wheels of motion.

Stillness became a dislocated home with no memory.

Convergence appeared as today's yearning for yesterday and tomorrow.

An equation asked for the combination of what wasn't and what can't be and thus created a dream of double negation: An invitation evoking the absence of pre-desire and post-satisfaction.

Here stillness became motion. We moved to avoid being one or two.

My dream was quite different. I watched heavenly lights transform themselves into the most beautiful sounds ever heard. At the end of this celestial concert, the lights arranged themselves into letters projected onto the evening sky. This is what I read in the sky:

> In the vibratory realm, notes know.
> Music meets where lines dare not go.
> Ever on and in between lie places never spoken.
> Here.
> Sound.

Neither one of us had ever written a poem in our entire life and to dream of a poem was the most unimaginable thing in our imaginations. From that moment on we decided to meet regularly in the open field. No matter how serious we found ourselves upon arrival, we soon forgot the troubles of the world and began running, skipping, and dancing. We began to believe we were reincarnated, lunatic, Sufi dancers.

Over the years we managed to build a huge, foolish project. We had it constructed several thousand times and you are now discovering that one of the arks we sent into the world is, this very moment, sitting in your hands.

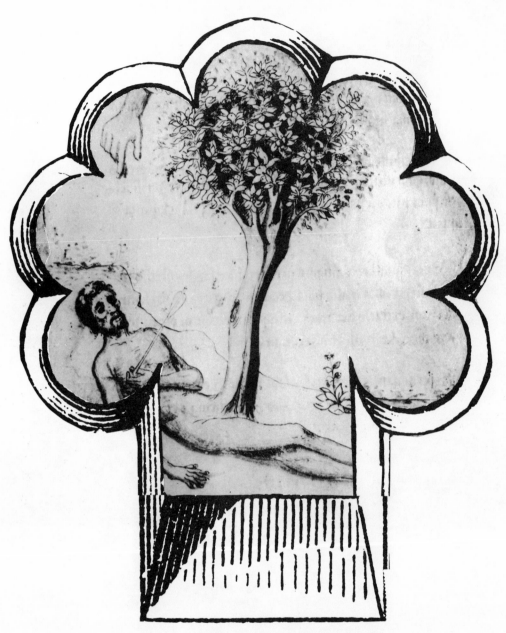

Inhale the helium.
It is the wind of the Gods.
It moves us toward the sleep
where we find ourselves awakened.

What is the Answer?

One morning while traveling on the freeway, I passed a billboard with this message printed in gigantic letters:

Go to the next filling station to get the answer.

My curiosity prevented me from driving on to my job. I could not resist finding out what the sign meant. I pulled off the next exit and turned into an old rusty gas station. It had a sign saying, GAS AND SASS. I got out and asked the attendant if he knew anything about the billboard on the highway. He said, "Yepper, that's what I get paid fer."

He went on to explain how an old woman had come by a month before and hired him to work at the run down station. He said the gas pumps didn't work and the only gas he sold was helium gas for balloons. He then gave himself a hit of helium and talked in a silly voice saying, "I love to sass when I get this gas." He started laughing so hard I thought he would kill himself with an overdose of merriment.

When he gathered his wits he returned to the story. He mentioned how the old woman was very rich and a bit crazy. She had told him she was a wealthy ghost who had received permission to come back to earth for one day. When asked why she had come back, she told him, "I am a Deadhead who has come back to give the answer."

The old man told me the old woman claimed to be Gertrude Stein. She hired him to put up the billboard sign and sit in the gas station with a tank of helium. Her instructions were to wait for the first person who came and sincerely asked about "the answer." "All I have to do now is give you the letter she left and then my job is done," the old man uttered as he took another gasp of helium.

Under the influence of helium the old rascal began singing, "Don't Fence Me In." He became so wildly amused with himself I thought he wouldn't live long enough to pass on the letter. But like the last time, he recuperated from his paroxysms of laughter and managed to walk over to the defunct gas pump. With a gigantic canyon of a smile he said, "Now it's time to really get you some sassy gas." He asked me to hold out my hands and then acted as if he were going to pump gas into my cupped palms.

"Oops, I almost forgot." He then carefully placed the gas pump on the ground and ran inside to get the helium tank. He rolled it out on a cart and said we each had to take a breath before the pump would work. To humor the old man I took a breath. He then took a monstrous dose and squeaked, "Now let's get some gas that will really sass." He asked me if I was ready for it and I responded that I was, in the goofiest voice I ever heard. I felt I was a ridiculous cartoon character and I couldn't stop laughing. That was when the old man started to get serious.

He pulled the trigger on that old gas pump like he was going to pour out liquid gold. Into my hands fell no gas or any fluid. What came out of that antique pump was a pink letter wrapped in purple ribbon. In the most beautiful writing the letter was addressed, "To the One Who Will Receive the Answer."

"That's it. Now the ball is in your court," the old man quickly spoke out. I hurriedly opened the letter and found "the answer" written as follows:

> There ain't no answer.
> There ain't going to be an answer.
> There has never been an answer.
> That's the answer.

The letter was signed, "Your faithful attendant of sass and gas, Gertrude Stein."

Soon after, I noticed the old man taking another hit of helium. He didn't stop with one breath or even two. He kept on sucking the gas until he began to lift right off the ground. Up into the sky he went, waving and laughing hysterically. He went so high I could no longer see him. I honestly don't know where that helium sucker went.

I do know that I quickly en- tered my vehicle and with great haste went about my business. For weeks I told no one about the answer received at the gas and sass stop. I was afraid they would think I had lost all my sanity.

Late one evening, two weeks after the incident, my phone rang. The call was from the old helium man. He asked, "Have you been thirsty for some more gas and sass?" After his laughter stopped, he said, "You see, I was really the ghost of Gertrude Stein. I had to make a balloon and keep myself full of helium so you would listen to me. I did a good job of convincing you, didn't I?" "Yes, Gertrude," I responded, going along with the trickster's prank.

Gertrude went on to say I would receive some more gas and sass in the morning, and she hoped I had some "good old fashioned helium dreams." That evening I dreamt of flying. I was a balloon at the Macy's Thanksgiving Parade and everyone in my dreams, people and animals alike, spoke with silly, helium-inspired voices.

When I woke up the next morning I discovered a tank of helium lying in the bed. I thought, "This is getting too damned weird! How did this get there?" When I pulled the tank out I noticed a note attached to it. The note directed me to look out the bedroom window. I turned toward the window and saw a string attached to a branch on the largest tree in the yard. The string was connected to a helium balloon floating high in the morning sky. I managed to get dressed and shot out to the garage, getting a ladder to reach the tree branch and pull down the balloon.

When I pulled on the balloon it popped and the air became filled with the sound of helium-laughter. A letter came falling down from the sky. I picked it up and read:

> *John Cage, a new member of the Helium Ghost Society, has asked me to tell you that "life is too important a thing to ever talk seriously about it."*
>
> *Your old gassed up geezer,*
>
> *G.S.*

A weird idea struck me at that very instant. It was so strange I couldn't believe it was me who thought it up. The idea was to write a letter to Gertrude and send it up into the sky via a helium balloon. Without wasting a second, I went to my desk and wrote this letter:

> *Dear Sass with Gass,*
> *Is it really you that is up there?*
>
> *Most Sincerely,*
>
> *An admirer*

I folded the letter, placed it in a balloon, filled it with helium, and up into the air it went until I no longer could see it. The next day I arose and raced toward my bedroom window. Low and behold there was a balloon in the sky attached by string to the tree branch.

When I pulled on the string, the balloon again burst and filled the sky with crazy laughter. Another letter fell to the ground. It was a one word reply: "Maybe."

I sent a second letter asking whoever was up there to tell me what I was supposed to do next. The next day a letter from the sky directed me to start paying more attention to the branch on the tree that held the balloon.

I went to the tree branch with a magnifying glass and carefully examined it. By this time nothing surprised me and it was not a shock to discover that the branch had a carved message on it. These words were beautifully etched onto it:

> Build yourself an air balloon the size of Noah's Ark. Take two photographs of every living creature on board with you. Release yourself into the sky and visit us in our gassy and sassy home.

Believe it or not, I dedicated my life to building this balloon. I sold everything I had and learned all the skills necessary to build it. Furthermore, I learned all that could be known about all the living creatures of the world.

On the summer evening of a full moon I went into the air with all the animals. I felt like Noah and I'm certain my neighbors thought I was as crazy as Noah's neighbors judged him to be. Up and up into the sky I went. As the air became thinner, I fell asleep and had a dream about being in a large boat at sea. When the storms in my dream began rocking the boat, I awakened. Right in front of my eyes stood the old man who called himself Gertrude Stein. He or she said, "Now that you have come, I can ask you to hear my confession. It will only take a minute. I cannot be released until someone who is sassy and gassy hears about my mistake."

This helium filled creature went on to explain how he had been too serious about life. Even his awareness of life's absurdities had been too seriously addressed. In the other worlds where physical bodies aren't used, this seriousness was a weight prohibiting him from escaping the pull of earth's gravity. The only solution for his release was to gain some more levity.

The old helium creature needed to return to earth in the form of a balloon ghost and create some levity in order to help him levitate toward higher dimensions of being. He had done this with me and to prove his success he had to convince me to do something weird, absurd, and bizarre.

As he said this, he began to float upwards into the heavens. "Thank you for your help. You won't be forgotten. The gods of levity have taught you how to fly as a token of their appreciation for helping me. Never forget that nothing in life is so serious that it can't be fixed with some sass and gas."

That was the last time I ever spoke with the old helium man who claimed to be Gertrude Stein. I must have fallen asleep again because the next thing I remembered was sitting in the middle of a field where two men were running around me, skipping and giggling like children. One of them had what appeared to be a tree branch wrapped with audio recording tape.

What they told me is another story, and, if my memory serves me right, you've already heard those helium inspired tales.

Open your mind so that
its contents may fall out.
This brings the emptiness that
enables a sacred filling to take place.

What is the Question ?

I once wrote a book entitled, *The Very Serious Guide to Enlightenment*. Before it was published, something happened that caused me to throw away the manuscript and radically change my life.

The story begins back in the fall of 1969. I had just graduated from high school and was getting ready for my freshman year in college. Being a very serious student, I was beginning a journey of finding all the right answers. That's what I had been taught an education was all about.

I enrolled in every serious course, carefully studying each world religion, each philosophy, and each science and system of mathematics. In this way I became a bank of memorized "right answers." I often made perfect scores on the exams and had a perfect grade point average.

I went right on taking all the courses in the university and graduated many years later with many advanced degrees. Soon after graduation my serious book on enlightenment was written and was ready to be sent to the publisher. I remember the morning I walked toward the post office to mail the manuscript. On the way I passed through a beautiful city park.

When I got to the central area of the park, I walked around a crystal clear lake and a beautiful lady with dark hair walked by. With a twinkle in her eyes she simply asked, "What do you know today?" Without thinking I automatically said, "Why nothing. Absolutely nothing at all." She smiled and I took notice of how surprised I was at my own answer. The words had just popped out of my mouth. I felt bewildered realizing that this was the only moment in my life when I felt, really felt, I had given the right answer.

I then added the remark, "Yes, it has taken me most of my life to learn that I know nothing. I hope I won't forget and have to learn it all over again." I had no idea where these words were coming from, but they rang of absolute truth. My whole world was turned upside down and I never arrived at the post office. I walked around the lake until it became dark and then went home and threw the manuscript away.

My initiation into the world of "not knowing" began that evening. Sitting in my living room chair I entered a relaxed state of being. I became very still, and it became possible to hear my own voice speak from the depths of my soul. Every night thereafter I attended this inner university where I taught myself to unlearn everything I had ever been taught. The education given to me at the university was shown to be a lie based on arrogance, greed, and vulgar social control.

It took a long while for me to get over my anger at the school systems, from elementary school through high school, college, and graduate school. They were all the same. Teachers taught one to give the right answer. In giving the right answer, we all became homogenized voices of complete predictability. A perfect test score meant one's responses were completely predictable. We had been programmed to stop inventing anything new and even worse, had accepted the routine as a holy interaction that could not be scrutinized or critically examined in any profound way.

I had actually written an extensive essay — a diatribe against modern education — and planned to put it at this point in this book. But I have thrown that text away too — it wasn't funny.

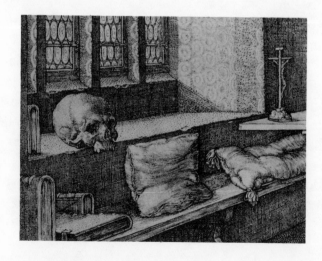

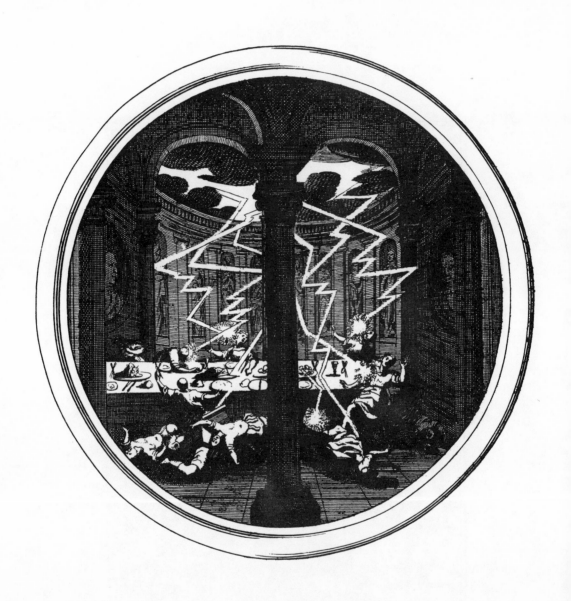

From the lightning came the skull.
In its rain came the wisdom
named crazy.

The Origin of the Crazy Wisdom Tales

Many centuries ago a young boy went into the forest to learn from its creatures. They taught him everything they knew. Even the lakes and streams taught him their vast reservoirs of knowledge and deep wisdom. Still not satisfied, the plants taught him to sing and the insects taught him how to dance. There was not one living creature who did not teach this little boy all they knew.

No matter how much the boy learned, he never felt grate-full enough. Using what he had been taught by the creatures, he summoned the great thunder clouds and asked them to teach him whatever was left to know. They said, "We must warn you. There is only one lesson you have not learned. Please do not ask us to teach you. We fear it will make you too full."

There was nothing that would stop this boy from asking for that final knowledge. When he made his last request, the great thunder beings cautiously asked him again if he was absolutely sure. The boy shouted, "You must teach me. I have to know everything!" The thunder beings began to rumble and the whole earth shook from their mighty force.

Within an hour the thunder beings filled the boy's mind with the suffering experienced by people throughout the world. The boy began to make rain with his own eyes and continued raining for one hundred years. After that time a lighting bolt struck him, instantly and violently killing him. All that remained on the ground was his dust neatly arranged as if it were a sand painting. What people saw was the image of a skull with a lightning bolt.

When the boy went to the spirit world he asked God why the thunder beings made him rain for so many years, only to be struck by a violent lighting bolt at the end of his life. God said, "You asked to know everything." They had to show you what you didn't know. You knew nothing about the world's suffering, its pain, and its struggles. Did you learn your lesson?"

The boy, now an old man, asked, "How could I learn anything if all I could do was make rain with my eyes?" God gently replied, "When you know everything, all you can do is weep in order to help heal the suffering of others." The man said, "God, you must invent something else that human beings can do other than raining tears and breaking their hearts. Please create another way of serving our brothers and sisters. Teach me and I will return to teach the human beings."

God had been a little bored with his own life and was engaged by the sincerity of this challenge. He decided to invent another way of healing the suffering associated with the human condition. He named this new medicine, "crazy wisdom," and this is what the man was taught by the Great Creator. God spoke these words to his new prophet:

"We will name this new knowledge crazy wisdom. It will be hidden by the sounds of ridiculousness and frivolity that surround it. In this way its powerful and sacred nature will be protected from all the dangerous inhumans. As you know, the dangerous ones are those who have not been taught by the animals, plants, insects, plants, and other creatures in my kingdom. They only pay attention to the idiotic games of so-called 'education.' They teach themselves to survive without an imagination.

"They begin their childhood with more wisdom than they have when they reach adulthood. By the time they are fully educated, they spend their lives helping maintain an archaic system of mental slavery. This is what makes the gods weep. We see our children perpetuating so much evil on one another under the guise of calling it 'good service.'

"I know you were taught about the evil perpetuated by the self-annointed 'do-gooders,' those who use the rhetorical devices of religion, therapy, education, and politics. These are the most dangerous ones. The so-called 'criminals' have always been closer to me than any of those 'do-gooding frankensteins.'

"I will place the holiest wisdom inside of that which people think is absurdity, nonsense, the ridiculous, and the irreverant. None of the serious monsters will ever see it, even if it's presented to them right in front of their very own eyes. It wouldn't matter if they heard this conversation. They could not possibly believe. Their minds have become so corrupted and bent into knotted entanglements that up is down, good is bad, bad is good, war is defense, and ignorance is education.

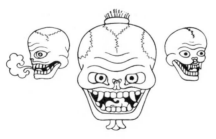

"Once I tried to humor these unenlightened ones by creating a devil. I made him as a joke, never believing anyone would take it seriously. I thought they knew the gods are only interested in joy, play, and love. Why would any parent want to create anything that would be so stupidly irritating to their children?

"These inhumans see everything in terms of pathology, sin and evil. They have become incapable of seeing how they see. It is they who paint the world darkly and then diabolically claim to see it with positive colorings as they go about claiming to know what is good for everyone else. They pathologize one another, particularly with those horrid linguistic messes called 'psychology' and 'education.' This creates forms of duplicitous terrorism the most vicious despot couldn't imagine inventing. All done, of course, under the guise of being good and serving others.

"This is why the gods weep. It is the professional teachers, therapists, doctors, lawyers, bankers, and politicians, that have most deeply hurt our creation. We once sent someone down to warn them that it would be as hard for them to enter our kingdom as it would be for a camel to pass through the eye of a needle. What did these people do? They invented theologians who found ways to muddle even the simplest stories of our holy messenger.

"I had given up, believing that only tears could help wash away the pain of those abused by all the 'good' people. But now you come along, the man who had to learn everything, and challenge me to try again.

"I have thought long and hard about your request. This is what we will do.

"I will send you back to earth with the assignment to destroy all the sacred institutions with winds of laughter. The laughter that brings forth tears will release the great cleansing floods. The quaking ignited by gigantic explosions of giggling will shake the very foundations of all these pious and pompous profess-anals. In this way we will end the world and prepare it for a new birth, the beginning of mirthful earth.

"We will call this invasion, Mirth Birth. You are to recruit secret agents to help you in this mission. For reasons of protection their names can not be revealed. Go bless these people to go forth into the world and destroy all seriousness. It is time for the world as we know it to end.

"I will send a sign when the great cleansing begins. Books will begin to appear praising the gifts of crazy wisdom, absurdity, and lunacy. They will be a most dangerous set of books, secretly directing how all serious institutions can be destroyed by wildness and sweet madness.

"At this time in the earth's history, the most effective pathway to enlightenment will be the path of lunacy. It will be almost impossible to progress through any traditional forms of seriousness. Sacred Clowns, Coyote Teachers, and Heyoka Healers will come out of the lakes and mountains to help stir the firmament of mirth. They will be known as the Reborn Deadheads and Very Merry Pranksters. These will be the last days and the beginning days.

"Go my son, for not a second more can be wasted on such serious talk. It's time for you to become wild and crazy in preparation for the holy crusade of crazy wisdom."

Overthrow the ungrateful demons of Seriousness.
Get on with the RA-volution of Egypt's golden
rays so that all that does not absurd
may be radiated by the light of dead.

Experimental Theatres of the Moment

When the angel of mirth came upon the earth, he began setting up what became known as "experimental theatres of the moment." This began as a new movement in the performing arts referred to as EXTM (pronounced "ex-TM"), but was actually the secret beginning of overthrowing the social plagues of seriousness and professionalisms. Enlightened Deadheads fully knew and appreciated the extent to which The Grateful Dead were part of this.

The basic idea was that people could interrupt their everyday habits by performing a little task, ritual, or prescription regarded as a form of experimental theatre. All these interspersed moments of theatre brought forth the absurd and ridiculous. In this way lunacy was inoculated into the nooks and crannies of people's everyday worlds.

Experimental Theatres of the Moment first began disrupting the profession of psychotherapy. People found themselves radically transformed by these enactments and the whole idea of therapy became obsolete in the same way kerosene lamps disappeared when electrical lighting was introduced. This was the beginning of the age of transformative enlightenment.

It wasn't long until people began creating their own forms of EXTM. Communities and neighborhoods became filled with all kinds of performing groups and designers of alternative experiences. Children and adults began understanding the foolishness of educational systems based on threat and torture and began acting out EXTM in the classrooms. In this way education, or at least the form of it which tortured human imagination, came to an end.

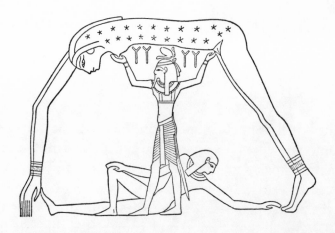

In this new age of creating minds, mystical mindfulness was reborn. Shamans were reinstated into the society as masterful improvisers of mental process. Musicians and poets replaced politicians and newscasters. Children were turned into teachers following the peaceful revolution of joy led by what the last of the serious historians called "the children's revolution." Adults were sent to playgrounds when they became too serious and those unable to withdraw from addictions to oneupsmanship were asked to live in the only prison on earth, Disneyworld.

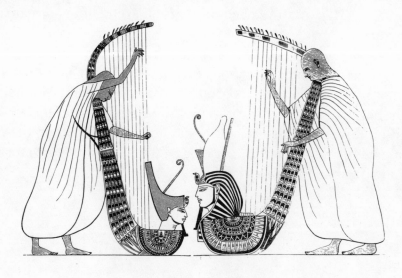

After the world was transformed by EXTM, the first peoples of the world, the indigenous elders from all over the planet were asked to be the custodians and leaders of Mother Earth. The world as we now know it completely disappeared. Twelve sacred tree branches were planted into the earth's spiritual center and the planet gave re-birth to the Garden of Evena. Nothing more can be said about it because too many people would panic if they realized the extent to which EVERYTHING is going to come down.

Only one additional item of information related to this story can be released. During the remodeling of Carnegie Hall, a message was found carved into the floor right on the spot where John Cage performed his first concert in the great hall. With a magnifying glass these words were clearly etched:

Theatre takes place
all the time,
wherever one is,
and art simply facilitates
persuading one
that this is the case.

Make a joyful noise.
The dissonance of its silence will erase the world.

Channeling Silence: Erasing the World

Toward the last days of the New Age Movement, or what became known as the Old New Age, almost every person had tried channeling. Ancient spirits, extraterrestrials, nonhuman forms, plants, and wild-life were all channeled in this final frenzy of entranced exploration. Thousands of books were published based on the words that came forth from channeling.

A time came when people began getting very tired of mediums and channelers. The moment was ripe for the emergence of one last great channeler. A book predicted the forthcoming of this metaphysical won-der. Within a year the awaited for enlightened being appeared and dem-onstrated the prodigious ability to psychically tap into the core of the whole universe and express its most holy silence.

Thousands of people were told by their personal spirit guides that the messenger of ancient wisdom had finally returned. This last great channeler was not in a human form, but in that of a small turtle, no more than five inches long. It carried a sacred branch on its shell and was brought to many auditoriums where multitudes of people witnessed the holy turtle's divine channeling of silence.

As a teacher the silent turtle helped many inhumans begin trans-forming themselves back into being human beings. In the presence of the holy turtle teacher they were able to spontaneously learn how to channel silence. Their former inner world, as they had previously known it, came to an end.

This is how god's angel of silence cleansed and ended our world, preparing the planet for the birth of mirthful earth.

Now is the time for all Deadheads
to sign their name.

Getting Ready

With some tape attach an extremely tiny piece of bark from a tree branch to this page. Sign your name underneath it. Over your signature write the signature, "Deadhead." Over the next month or two find four other people who have read this book and have prepared their bark. Do not turn to the next page of this book until all of you, a total of five, have found one another and come together for this occasion. If you can't find four other people, then prepare four people by giving them a gift wrapped copy of *Crazy Wisdom Tales for Deadheads*. Tell them to call you when they get to the page in the book that tells them to call.

MESSAGE TO READER:

If you were given this book as a gift, proceed to call the person who gave it to you.

When the group of five are prepared and assembled together, all may now turn the page at the same time and climb to the top story.

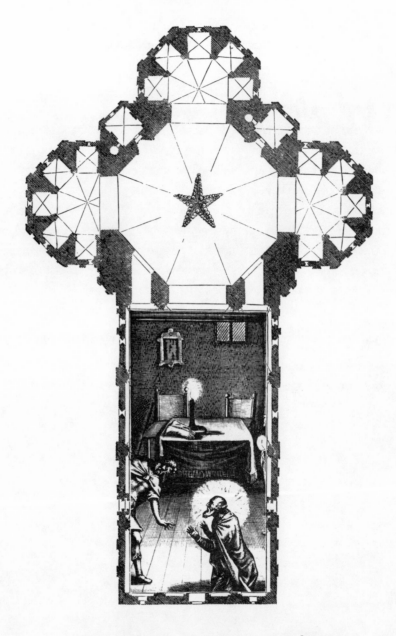

Become the final beacon of light.
Absurd yourself into every cranny
of the new world's fanny.

The Final Beacon

There was a different time in another dimension where five other individuals climbed a multi-storied temple of Deadhead enlightenment. When they began reading the final story, they read about you who are now reading about them. In this story, some directions were given which the readers, particularly you, had to follow in order to make the story become more than a story. Here are the final directions:

Each of you is to gather your sacred tree branch and attach it to the other branches with string, making a five-sided pentad. When the pentad is constructed carry it to an open field. Place it in the center of the field and dance around it in a completely ridiculous fashion. Make certain you get some hopping, skipping, and backwards jogging into this dance.

When your dance is complete, bury the pentad in the center of the field. Take one teaspoon of soil from the burial sight for each group member. Thank the sacred branches for helping take you to the top. Immediately depart from the field.

Purchase five flashlights, one for each group member. Open the end where the lightbulb is located and place your soil from the sacred burial ground into it. Make certain each flashlight is armed with fresh batteries and is in good operating order after instilling the soil.

All of you are to take these specially prepared flashlights to the highest point you can find in your community. It is best if this spot is in a natural area and the task performed in the evening. Find the right spot and turn each flashlight on, aiming it up toward the heavens. Place the flashlights in the ground so they stand straight up and continue shining into the sky. Arrange them so they make the figure of the pentad you previously buried in the open field.

In the center of this pentadic beacon place a copy of *Crazy Wisdom Tales for Deadheads*. Make certain its inside is inscribed with these words:

We made it to the top and so can you!

Sign each of your names and wrap the book in aluminum foil before placing it into the center of the light. When this is done all of you should say these words together:

We are the final beacon of light.
Let us go back into the world
and transform it
with shamanic absurdity.

Immediately depart and celebrate your climb to the top with a great feast. Agree to meet once a year to exchange stories about the ways in which you introduced more absurdity into the world.

If each of you faithfully commits to continuing this journey for the rest of your life, then one or more of these events will probably happen to you in this lifetime:

+ A library book will fall on your head.
+ You will find yourself writing messages on tree branches and leaving them in libraries and bookstores.
+ At least once every three years you will make a pilgrimage to a special lake, stream, or body of water and baptize yourself with its holy drops.
+ Ibn 'Arabi will come to you in a dream or you will find yourself writing his initials on book margins for no apparent reason.
+ You will begin writing poems, drawing unusual symbols, and making collections of weird things to display in your home.
+ You and your friends will exchange recipes for cooking up some

weirdness. One day your collection will be complete enough to be produced as a community cook book of communed weirdness.

+ A small tank of helium will sit in your living room.

+ You will send twelve copies of R. D. Laing's book, *Knots*, to twelve teachers of psychotherapy with this inscription: *Please untie your own shoestring whenever you think of knotting the knots of others. This is not about creating another knot of pathology, but a notting of other psychological knots.*

+ You will write at least one letter to God.

+ The letters "EXTM" are a bumper sticker on your car.

+ A turtle shell with a branch on it adorns the entrance to your abode.

+ You never make an important decision without sleeping on a piece of tree bark.

+ At least five times you leave grafitti that looks like a pentad with these words in the center: *Prepare for the big laugh.*

Should you ever wake up in the middle of the night and see yourself beholding the multi-storied Temple of Deadhead Enlightenment, you will know that a great and ridiculous shamanic guide is sitting outside your window shining a specially designed flashlight into your eyes. Do not look into this light for longer than a second. If you look or even think about this happening to you for longer than one second, your mind will empty and become vulnerable to the chuckling winds of enlightenment.

I once looked for longer than a second and immediately heard a story about the beings who published this book. Once upon a time they were the spirits of the moon, the luna ones. Wanting to visit the earth they transformed themselves into creatures with wings. Some of them came to the earth as luna moths and others settled into the form of the sacred loon.

Their Goddess, Susan, had an extraordinarily beautiful soul and could see into the hearts of all living creatures. She was originally the brightest star in the heavens, but the gods split her into two points of holy light. One light was carried in her own heart and the other was allowed to journey through the mystical hearts of enlightened beings. When she arrived on earth, the magicians and alchemists periodically captured this roaming light and made it the mystical silver used in alchemy. This alchemical element came to be called *luna*.

Eventually the luna ones were recruited by god's own angel of lunacy. This angel was given the earth name "George" and was referred to as "Dr. Q" by the gods who sent him. He came to earth disguised as a brilliant poet with great mystical gifts. The spirits wed him with the luna Queen and gave them the task of starting a printing press. They gave birth to many books having alchemical effects of radical transformation on anyone who read them.

All the luna ones want you to know that now is the time for all Dead-heads — *all those who know they are Deadheads and all those who haven't yet realized they are Deadheads* — to begin rewriting the stories of your next life. This new life of Deadhead enlightenment began the second you entered this book. As you become more devoted to doing really weird things, you will help shake the center of earth herself! In this way we will awaken the dead and fulfill the prophecy of the Great Collaboration:

> *The stick of which we have spoken,*
> *at perhaps tiresome length,*
> *is never straight.*
> *If you toss it like a baton from hand to hand,*
> *it never repeats itself.*
> *If you wave it like a beacon in the night air,*
> *you hear what is never spoken.*

> **George Quasha,**
> ***Somapoetics***

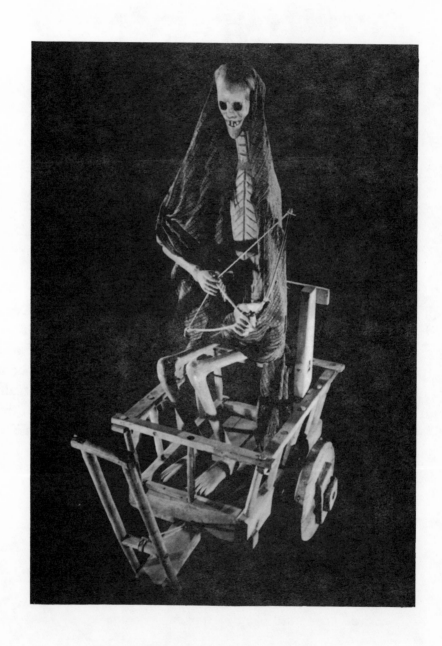

More Merry Pranks

Seven

Have someone take a photograph of you reading the sentence you are now reading. When the picture is developed, write this caption on it: *"Obeying my Shamanic Companion to the Grateful Dead."*

Eight

Purchase a brand new pencil. In a private place talk to the pencil, asking it to help you become enlightened. Sharpen the pencil and keep it in a safe place. Only use this pencil to write the word "enlightenment." Every day write this word at least once with the pencil, but never more than twelve times. Do this until it is impossible to hold the pencil any more.

When it is no longer possible to write with the pencil, place it in a small box and seal it. On the top of the box write these words, "The Silent Pencil." Every night before going to sleep get out the box and shake it like a rattle. Say the word "enlightenment" twelve times while you are rattling the silent pencil. Do this until you have a dream about being enlightened.

Nine

Tape record yourself saying the word, "enlightenment" in as many ways as you can. Vary the volume, pitch, rhythm, tone, coloring, and general feeling of your voice. Try different pronunciations of the word. Whisper it. Shout it. Stutter it. Say it while running your fingers over you lips. Say it with water in your mouth. Say it while you're winded from exercise. Say it while thinking of other words. Say it in different parts of the room. Say it so it can not be heard.

When you have a tape of all the possible ways you can imagine saying "enlightenment," proceed to unwind the tape from the audiocassette. Wrap the tape around your house or dwelling place prior to going to sleep. Get up the next morning before the sun rises and wrap the tape around a tree branch.

Hang this wrapped branch on the wall next to your bed. Write a sign underneath it with this caption, "My staff of enligtenment." Allow a week to go by so your staff can get energized by your unconscious dreams.

At the end of the week, remove the staff from the wall and go to a country field. Run around the field in large circular patterns while holding the enlightened staff high above your head. Imagine you are enlightening the field with this staff.

Pretend the staff not only enlightens the field, but also enlightens you. What would you do with this staff if this really happened? Think carefully about answering the question. Would you build a special place for the staff? Would you donate it to a museum? Would you give it to the person you care most about?

When you are certain about your response, consider that if you actually did this to your staff, the staff would gather the power necessary to enlighten you. Under no circumstance are you to do anything to your staff unless you have fully reckoned with living with the consequences of possibly becoming enlightened.

Ten

Have a friend take twelve photographs of you. The first photograph should be of you looking as unenlightened as you possibly can look. Change each pose to look as if you are becoming more enlightened. The last photographs should reveal the look of a completely enlightened being.

Frame this series of photographs and caption it, "The Evolution of Deadhead Enlightenment." Hang it on your bedroom wall so you see it when you are lying in bed.

For the next twelve days you are to use this series of photographs to direct your conduct. On day one, take out the first photograph and carry it with you. Try to look like this photograph as many times as you can during the first day. Act, look, feel, talk, see, and hear like the person photographed. Do the same for each photograph throughout the next twelve days.

Keep a diary of how each day was experienced. Title this diary, *The Twelve Day Story of Creating Deadhead Enlightenment*. Place this diary book in your bedroom near the photograph gallery.

For the next twelve months begin your day by looking at the photographs and deciding which level of enlightenment you want to exhibit for the day. Read the diary book to remind yourself how that level was experienced and go through the day trying to enact it. Keep daily notes for each day in a new diary titled, *Advanced Tips for the Successful Exhibition of Various Degrees of Deadhead Enlightenment*.

Eleven

Write your life story up to the present point. Allow yourself the necessary time to do this job. Do not write a psychological analysis of any of your life experiences. Tell your story from the perspective of someone who is becoming enlightened. Assume you will be enlightened in the future and that future readers will be interested in the events in your past that may have contributed to this enlightenment.

When you are caught up to the present time, make up the rest of your life story. Create a future specifying the way you want to become enlightened and the difference this makes in how you live.

Wrap this book in birthday wrapping paper and place it in a storage locker. Every year on your birthday go to the locker, unwrap it, and read it. Rewrap the autobiography and place it back in the locker until next year's birthday.

Twelve

Gather twelve boxes of different sizes. Make certain your head can fit into each one of them. Cut a hole in each box enabling a flashlight to fit and shine upon your eyes when the box is placed over your head.

In the evening of a full moon place each box over your head for one minute per box. Make certain the light shines upon your eyes. Close your eyes while you are in the box world.

Repeat this procedure whenever there is a full moon. Do not use the flashlight or the boxes for any other purpose. One evening the light will go off. When that happens take it as a sign that the appropriate box has been chosen. Get rid of all the other boxes.

Continue using this box and the burned out light whenever there is a full moon. Wait until you are able to begin imagining the presence of an inner light that can illumine the burned out light. You may catch a glimpse of this light while you are in the box or while you are in your dreams. When you think you have caught a glimpse of the imagined light, stop using the box. Place the box in a secret storage area and feed it one light bulb on every full moon. Believe that every bulb given to it helps your inner light become brighter. Fill the box with light bulbs and think about all the potential light in the box prior to going to sleep every night.

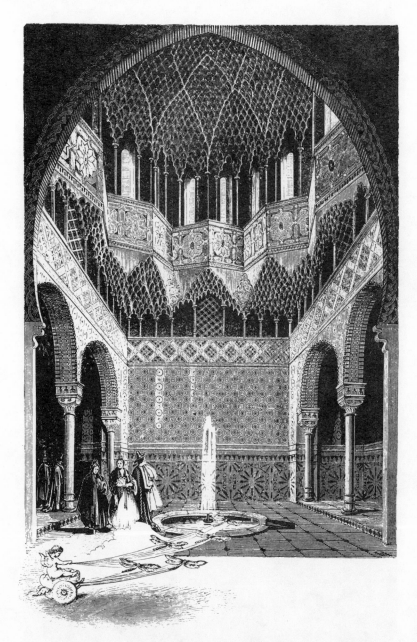

Here lie the stones, the words, the shapes,
and the dreams.
Give them to all the children
so they may raise us Dead.

After Words

Licking the Air:
Speaking the Lost Tales of the Original Kin
(*Children's Stories for Little Deadheads*)

GRANDFATHER'S SACRED STONES

There was a time in my life when I wasn't sure about magic. Even when I doubted, there was one thing I was certain about. Without a question, I knew my grandfather, PaPa, was the most magical human being I had ever known. He always had a trick up his sleeve, whether it was a secret noisemaker or a silly joke catching you offguard. I still remember how he used to hide behind doors and jump out to surprise the family dog. No one escaped his crazy world of merriment, not even the household pets!

PaPa did have his serious moments. Nothing was more serious than when he went up to the attic to open his old black trunk. Although he hadn't traveled outside this country, his trunk looked like it had been around the world. I never got to see all the things in the trunk, but I knew there were secrets and mysteries in it. My sister and I would sometimes sneak into the attic to touch the trunk and wonder about its locked contents. Our PaPa pretended he didn't know we were up there, but we knew he knew and that he enjoyed our being completely mystified by his old trunk.

There is a memory from my childhood that haunts me to this day. It took place when I was spending a summer weekend with my grandparents. In the middle of a particularly quiet night PaPa got up and went toward the attic. The creaking sound of that old attic door awakened me and I immediately knew where he was going.

I quietly arose from my bed and tiptoed to the door in the hall lead-
ing to the attic stairs. I could hear his footsteps up above me. They
suddenly stopped and the rattling of an old key on the trunk sounded
through the still evening air. I nervously listened to the slow deliberate
whining of the trunk's lid being opened. "If I could only see what was
in that trunk," I thought to myself. "What does PaPa have that is such
a secret?"

I then heard PaPa sing a song that was unlike anything I had heard
before. He sang a simple song, almost like a child's song, but it sounded
very serious. It didn't have any words I could recognize, although I do
remember hearing something like, "Ho Ho Hee Oh." When PaPa stopped
singing, he began speaking. He said very slowly and distinctly, "Hello,
Grandfathers. Thank you for watching over my family." And then I
heard the song again with the "Ho Ho Hee Oh." He stopped and spoke
once more, "Grandfathers, help us be a good family." And he continued to sing that song.

He went on and on with this until he finally stopped. The house
became very still. A crackling sound began to fill the silence, the kind
of sound you hear when you place your ears next to a bowl of Rice
Krispies freshly soaked with milk. The crackling became louder and
louder and I became worried. Was the house's electrical wiring going
out of control? Had PaPa gotten shocked by some loose electrical wires?

I couldn't stand it any longer and ran up the stairs yelling, "PaPa,
PaPa, are you all right?" When I got to the attic, my heart almost stopped
and my forehead broke out with a heavy downpour of perspiration.
PaPa was lying on the floor with his eyes closed. I was just about to
scream, believing he had died, when he spoke. "It's all right my little
one. Sit down and listen to what the Grandfathers have to say."

He closed his eyes and the crackling sound started all over again.
The room began to glow in the area where PaPa was lying. I went closer
and saw his right hand open. He had four stones in it. These stones
were glowing with a bluish colored light. It was the stones making that
electrical sound. "How can a stone be electrical?" I thought outloud.

A voice that didn't sound like my grandfather quietly but authorita-
tively said, "Bob, sit down and listen to what your Grandfather wants

you to know." I immediately sat down with my back to the trunk. I moved my leg over so my foot would be touching the bottom of my PaPa's foot. It felt safer that way.

"We are the Grandfathers your PaPa keeps in the trunk. We are the stones you see in his right palm. Over the years we have taught those who are willing to listen and able to see. This seeing comes from a sincere heart and not from a doubting mind. Your grandfather has a pure heart and a sincere mind. This has made him very special to us. Because we have such great respect for how he respects our ways, we have granted him a wish. He has asked that we be introduced to you."

I looked at my PaPa who was still lying flat on the floor. His eyes were still closed, but I could see a smile on his face. Tears were flowing down his cheeks so I knew this was a very important moment.

The magical stones then lifted themselves right up into the air, slowly floating out of PaPa's hand. They came to the center of the room directly in front of me. PaPa began singing his song again and the stones began dancing in the air. They spun around one another, building up faster and faster speed with each orbit. As they sped up, the electrical crackling sound became louder.

PaPa then sang the words I had become familiar with, "Ho Ho Hee Oh, Ho Ho Hee Oh." He repeated this four times and then blew out a large breath of air. As difficult as this is to imagine, each of those stones flew to a different corner of the attic at the moment PaPa blew out his breath. Within seconds a rumbling was felt in the floor and it was obvious something big was going to happen. With the flash and explosion of a lightning bolt, the four stones came hurling straight toward one another. A great collision of these four stones was going to take place right in front of my eyes. I started to close my eyes and duck but something held me back. Maybe the presence of PaPa's calmness helped assure me that everything was going to be all right.

The four stones did collide. At the precise moment of impact, the attic changed itself into the most beautiful and mysterious place I had ever seen. It looked like we were in outer space and there were thousands, maybe millions of tiny meteor lights flying around us. The air crackled with energy and the strangest thing of all was that I had absolutely no fear as I sat and watched this amazing light show.

I'm not sure how long this lasted but it was not the same kind of clock time we are used to in our everyday lives. I might have been there five minutes or five days. That will always be a mystery.

The next thing I remember was lying in the middle of PaPa's living room covered with a blanket. PaPa was sitting in his chair next to me. He was drinking his coffee and reading the morning paper like he always did. He was wearing a perfectly starched white shirt, suspenders, and a bow tie. It was the way I usually saw him every morning.

"Had it been a dream?" I wondered. If so, it was the wildest, most real dream I had ever experienced. I was hesitant to say anything to PaPa. He might start teasing me about it and I was in no mood to be teased that morning. The dream had been too real.

"I fixed your breakfast," PaPa quickly said, before I could determine what I would say to him. "It's on the kitchen table." PaPa and I always got up several hours earlier than everyone else in the family and he usually fixed my breakfast. "Thanks PaPa," I quietly spoke. "Did you have a good night's rest?" I sheepishly added. He laughed and said, "Why I think I'll never forget it." I wondered what he meant by that.

I went to the kitchen and saw my glass of orange juice next to a white plate. There was no food on the plate. A leather pouch and a letter were sitting on the plate. I opened the letter and it had the following words written on it:

My Dear Grandson,

I introduced you to our Grandfathers last night. It was all true. The mystery and magic of our time together will live in your mind for the rest of your life. There are some things you must know. You are to be aware that someday you will also find four stones. I can't tell you how you will find them, but you will know them when you see them. They are out there waiting for you. Place your stones in this pouch and keep them in a trunk or old suitcase. Never let anyone else see them unless you intend to pass them on. You will be taught many other things in the future.

When I die, you will have these grandfathers to watch over you. We are never to discuss this again. I am not able to tell you any-

thing else about what took place last night. But I can tell you what my magic stones told me. They said it is time for me to teach you how to be a trickster. Starting today, you will be initiated into the family tradition of being an ambassador of great humor. I've waited all of your life to tell you this. I want you to know that this is a great moment in my life and our relationship with one another will never end, even when one or both of us is no longer on this planet as human beings. I can't tell you anymore at this time, but I can say that some day we will dance together just like you saw the stones dance. In someone else's attic or dark place, you and I will bring forth the whole universe. And that's a fact, my grandson. Always remember the grandfathers and thank them for the light they bring into our lives.

Your devoted grandfather, PaPa

The boy in this story grew up and many years after my PaPa died, I found my magic stones. I now have my own son who is preparing to receive this great mystery. That's it for now. I've told you all I can tell.

100 ♣ A Shamanic Companion to the Grateful Dead

THE SECRET WORDS OF AUNT ELIZABETH

Aunt Elizabeth was not like any other aunt. She lived by herself in an old two-story house and all the walls in every room were filled with books. There were new books, worn out old books, and ancient books that looked like they belonged to a museum. I have no idea how Aunt Elizabeth found the time to find all those books, let alone read them. You name the topic and she had a book on it, whether it was rare frogs of the Amazon or cooking secrets of the Egyptians.

The weirdest thing about Aunt Elizabeth was the way she had me do strange things with her books. For instance, she would ask me to find the book with the most interesting cover on it. She would give me one hour to find a book cover I liked, but she wouldn't allow me to open the book and read it. I would have to give her the book and she would wrap it with the most beautiful gift wrapping I'd ever seen and say, "You can't open this book until next year."

Sure enough, a year later Aunt Elizabeth would arrange for me to visit her and after serving one of her spectacular seven-layer cakes, the book would appear all nicely wrapped. She would sit down with me and read the book out loud. She would only allow the reading to take place for one hour. At the end of that time, she would say, "We need to take our time with this one. We don't want to get too full." And away the book would go to some hiding spot.

Over the years of my youth, there were many books my Aunt and I read together in this way. She played many games with me that always had the same outcome. I would always, one way or another, end up selecting a book that had some special meaning to us. The book would get whisked away, wrapped up, and only read at a future date in small portions.

Now you can begin to appreciate how different and special my aunt was. She loved her books and she enjoyed finding as many different ways as she could to get me interested in the mysteries they contained.

One morning at breakfast she asked my brother whether he had placed a book underneath his pillow. He thought she was kidding, but she asked everyone that morning whether they had ever tried this. When we asked her why she was asking us this question, she replied, "The answer is in a book. See if you can find it."

The entire summer was spent trying to get Aunt Elizabeth to give us a clue about the book that contained the secret answer as to why anyone should sleep with a book underneath their pillow. One day she gave us a clue. She said the book was the true story of a famous man who once slept with a book under his pillow. He grew up to be very famous as a man of many mysteries.

My brothers and sisters immediately began going through all her books, writing down the names of those that were biographies and autobiographies of famous people. There were many of these books in her house. Famous actors, doctors, writers, sports figures, leaders, and even rock musicians. How were we to choose the right name?

We were almost ready to give up when Aunt Elizabeth said, "Why I see you have found the book. It's one of the titles you wrote down." This gave us new hope and inspiration. We asked if it was a man or a woman. "Fair question," she replied. "It's a man who lived in the United States during this century." Although this helped reduce our list, the number of titles on it was still way too long for us to believe we could find it before the end of summer.

During the middle week in August, we still hadn't found the book. We decided to tell her we had given up. Aunt Elizabeth distracted us by telling us to watch the sky that evening because there was going to be a great meteor shower. As we sat in her backyard watching the stars shoot across the sky, she began telling us a story. She said it was a true story about a little boy who one day, while reading a book about a woman named Manoah, looked up and saw a mysterious woman. He didn't know who she was, but the woman told him to tell her what he wanted so she could grant it to him.

He responded, "I want to help others and especially help children when they're sick." When he told his mother about this story, she told him that he had been reading too much. When she realized that her son had truly had an experience that touched him deeply, she said, "Well these things sometimes do happen. It even says so in our religious books." She told her son that he was fortunate to be visited by such a magical person.

That same week the boy was having trouble in school. He couldn't remember the right answers from his school books. One evening he placed his school book underneath his pillow and thought about the woman who came to visit him. The very next morning he woke up to find he could remember every word in the book. He did this with the other books he had and sure enough, he remembered every word.

We asked our aunt whether this was really a true story and she insisted it was. She said the story was in the book they were trying to find. At that time she told us the boy's name. It was "Edgar Cayce." It didn't take us longer than a day to find that man's biography. We read the whole book to each other that week and it was an amazing story. We learned how he grew up and helped many people, particularly those who were sick. Believe it or not, he did this work in his sleep. For me, the most incredible thing about the book was how I never forgot a single detail about the summer it took to find it.

Now I want to tell you about Aunt Elizabeth's secret words. Not only did she have a house full of books, she had a house full of words. I'm not talking about the words printed in all those books. She literally had words written on small pieces of paper that were placed all over the house. She called these her "secret words."

Whenever my brothers and sisters tried to ask what these words meant, she would always say, "It's a secret, but I bet you can figure out the meaning." We looked the words up in every dictionary and encyclopedia in her house. Although we built quite a vocabulary we were never able to understand what the secret words were about.

I grew up to be a writer and not a week has gone by without my thinking of my Aunt Elizabeth's "secret words." I especially think about them when I'm writing books for young people.

A clue to their meaning came to me last year in a dream. Although my Aunt died years ago, I dreamed she was coming to visit me. In the dream she sent a letter asking me to prepare some "secret words" for her so she would feel at home. I don't know why I did this, but the very next day I carefully selected some "secret words" and placed them throughout my house. It didn't make any sense, but it made me feel good. It made me feel grateful for the magical presence my aunt had been to me and how much she influenced my life as a writer.

I'm writing this story to you at this very moment because last week I returned from a trip to Germany to visit the place where the famous Grimm brothers wrote their fairy tales. While I was strolling through a beautiful green German forest, I met a very old woman who resembled, in several ways, my Aunt Elizabeth. She spoke both German and English and came right up to me and asked if she could have a conversation.

We found a lovely spot underneath a huge tree on the edge of a lake whose surface looked like a perfect mirror. She told me that years ago she met a magical little girl who gave her a letter. The little girl told this German woman that she was never to open the letter. She was to always carry it with her. In the future she would meet someone in the woods who would be an adult woman. She would recognize this woman because her face would be similar to the little girl's features. She would have the same kind of nose, a dimple on each cheek, and a freckle on the bottom of her right ear lobe.

When the old German woman saw me she knew I was the person she had been waiting for. We sat down and told each other all about our lives. I told her about my aunt and her "secret words." We became so interested in sharing stories that I almost forgot about the "mystery letter." The old woman finally gave it to me and I nearly fainted when I opened it. This is what it said:

> My Dear Niece,
>
> If you are reading this letter, then you will have found the secret to my "secret words." A very long time ago, my own aunt gave me a letter telling me I should write down every word that is connected to any mystery in my life. Whenever I felt something mysterious or magical, I was to go to the nearest book and open it. I was instructed to write down the first word my eyes would read and place it on a small piece of paper.
>
> As I began doing this, more and more mysterious experiences began coming into my life. This is how I ended up with so many books and with so many words.

Now you must be wondering why my aunt told me to do this. She said, "If you never tell anyone what I'm telling you, then a very special person in your future will be able to use the magic that these secret words will have accumulated. The mystery and magic in these words and books will open her mind to the mystery of all words and books. In this way you will be helping this special person become a famous writer."

I write this letter with the hope that everything my aunt told me was true. If you have found this letter then you will know that she told me the truth. You will also know that I told you the truth about magic and mystery in the world of books. Please remember me as you decide whether you will start your own collection of secret words.

Love,
Aunt Elizabeth

I never stopped writing secret words from that day onward. My house is now filled with many books and many secret words. Perhaps you will see me in your own day-dreams or night-dreams. If you do so, simply say to me, "I know you are a gift of mystery."

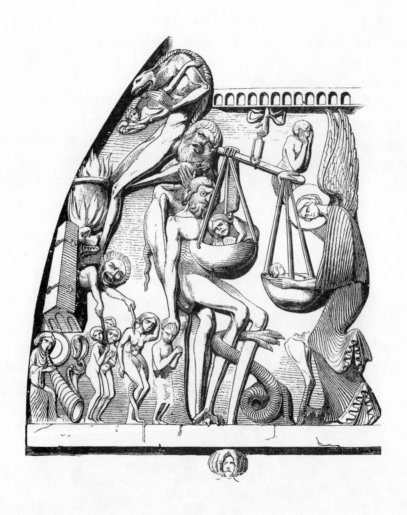

SHAPE-SHIFTING

When the alarm went off that morning, I woke up thinking it would be another typical Tuesday school day. Looking back, I remember my fourth grade teachers, smiling and greeting us like they always did every school morning. I still remember their announcement at the beginning of that day, telling us there would be a special guest coming to visit our class after lunch.

At the time I had no idea that what would take place in the afternoon would be one of the most amazing afternoons of my life. You see, parents and other guests often came into our class and taught brief courses on many subjects, like cooking, wood carving, poetry, and drama. We were familiar with those experiences. But on that Tuesday afternoon on October 12, something very strange and unexplainable took place.

It began the moment the guest arrived at 1:00 in the afternoon. He was an old man with white hair and a long white beard. Resting on top his head was a well worn white hat with four small bells attached around its brim. When he had entered the classroom and sat down, the door slowly closed and then opened again by itself. Everyone looked at one another and thought, "Did that really happen?" When he opened the old suitcase he had brought with him, a cool breeze circled the room and was felt across the back of every youngster's neck.

He was silent for a few very long moments, causing me to drift my attention toward the outside window. I noticed how the clouds were moving quickly, more quickly than I had ever seen them move. As my thoughts were lost in the sky, the man began to speak and it startled me, almost making me jump out of my seat. He talked very little, but I'll never forget a word he spoke.

"Today," he said, "I am going to tell you a great secret. I will only tell it this one time and then I will never speak about it again. That is all I'm required to do.

"I am going to tell you about shape-shifting. Shape-shifting is the ability to change your shape into the shape of something else. When I was a young boy, my grandfather told me how all his relatives knew how to turn themselves into many animals such as birds, wolves, deer, otters, buffalo, lions, and leopards. When you shape-shift, it is possible to turn yourself into anything. Why, I guess you could even turn yourself into a car or a school bus if you tried."

At that moment, my friend, Paul, became so excited he could no longer control himself. Stomping his feet and waving his arms, he shouted, "What do we have to do to shape-shift? Would you please tell us how to do it?"

There was a long nervous silence followed by what sounded like a high buzzing sound and four clicks. "I can only tell you if you ask," the old man replied. "Since you have asked, I must tell."

The old man slowly and cautiously reached into his ancient suitcase. You could hear the movement and noise of all kinds of things in that suitcase. He finally pulled out an old drum and a curved stick that looked like a snake.

"First," he said, " you must play a round drum like this one. Mine was made by a woman in the high mountains of South America. He then began to beat the drum in a powerful way. The more he beat that drum, the sleepier every boy and girl became. Each beat seemed to pound one deeper into a late night feeling. The beats began sounding like the heartbeat of someone deep in sleep.

The whole class was going into a magical trance as the drum kept on beating. He went on to say, "The curved stick that looks like a snake will help you shape-shift. It is not just a stick, but a rattle made by a Sioux Indian teacher from Pine Ridge, South Dakota. It has a leather pouch on its end that looks like the head of a snake. The pouch is filled with very special stone pebbles that are very old and holy. We call these stones our 'grandfathers.' When we shake this rattle, the grandfather stones help us shape-shift.

"What is most important for you to know is that you have to really want to believe you can shape-shift. You must imagine yourself becoming the thing you want to change your shape into. If you want to shift into being a wolf, then your mind, your vision, your hearing, your heart, and your feelings must become like that of the wolf.

"I'm now going to shake the rattle. As you hear the grandfather stones speak, I want everyone in this room to shape-shift into being your best friend." Within seconds I looked at my best friend who was sitting right next to me and thought, "Can this really happen? How will I change into him?" And then the rattle began to shake. And it shook and shook. The old man spoke, as if he were speaking directly to me, "Let your mind, vision, hearing, heart, and feelings become this other person. Let yourself dissolve into shifting your shape."

Slowly, but surely, I felt my face and body change to become that of my best friend. Without a doubt, it was a whole new world. I looked around and found I could see, hear, and feel different things. I was curious to find whether anything felt the same.

The man then said, "We're going to shape-shift again. This time I want everyone in the room to shape-shift into becoming your teacher." Everyone giggled at first, but when he shook that rattle, sure enough, every single student felt they could see, hear, think, and understand as their teacher. All the boys and girls were amazed at how different the school was when they saw it through the eyes of their teacher. They began to understand how challenging and difficult it was to be their teacher.

"Now," the old man said, "we're going to change into something that will really surprise you. Each of you will shapeshift into your favorite library book. Choose any book you want and when you hear the rattle, allow yourself to become that book."

One of the students, Tyler, shouted out, "How can we do that?" Another student, Brad, responded, "A book isn't a person!" "This one has got to be impossible," piped in their friend, Ben. The old man carefully picked up a book and said, "Each book contains a whole world of living things, places, and ideas. Each of you already knows how a book can take you to another world when you allow it."

He then shook the rattle in his special way and the students, every one of them, began turning into their favorite library books. One book said outloud, "I have met many friends and I love being held by them. When these friends of mine enter my world, I also enter their world." Another book also spoke out, "We books have always been shape-shifters. We shift people's realities all the time. Sometimes, when you forget you're reading, we can take you to a baseball park, a concert

Crazy Wisdom Tales for Deadheads ✦ 109

stage, to the moon, another galaxy, around the world, into the past, and into many different futures."

All the students were truly amazed to learn what the world was like from the view of being a book. They were learning far more than they ever thought was possible to know at school.

The old man then said he would shift us one final time. He told us to go stand by the windows of the classroom and look at the sky. I had a feeling something very important was about to happen. The rattle began to shake wildly as he spoke in a soft and melodic voice, "I want each of you to become the whole sky and allow yourself to shape-shift into it." The rattling became louder and louder and the sound of wind entered the classroom.

I cannot say what really happened at that moment. I do know that all of us felt like we left the classroom and dissolved into the whole sky. As the sky, we looked down at the school and saw it as a tiny dot on the earth. As the sky, we all felt the same. We honestly and truly felt like one big person. It was an amazing experience and it was the most amazing experience of my life.

The sound of wind was soon heard again along with the sound of bells. I wondered whether those were the bells from the old man's hat. Each of us slowly began to shapeshift back into being who we usually are. All of us were sleepy, and when I looked around, I found everyone rubbing their eyes to wake up.

When we were all fully alert, we discovered that the old man with white hair and a long white beard was no longer there. Our teacher ran to see if he was in the hall, but he was not there or anywhere. Scott and his friends, however, noticed a tiny message scribbled on the lower corner of the blackboard. It stated, "I have left you a letter. It is inside the desk of one of your teachers." With all the children cheering her on, the teacher quickly opened her desk, found the letter, and opened it. This is what the letter said:

My Dear Fourth Graders,

Once upon a time, I belonged to the sky. It was my family. In the same way you experienced being the sky, I, too, was once the sky.

As a young child, my grandfather taught me how to shape-shift. One day while shape-shifting, I turned myself into a human being. It was so interesting being a human being I couldn't stop trying all the things people do. I played baseball and basketball, read books, went to school, listened to music, and all the other things people enjoy. I became older and older until my hair turned as white as a cloud. It wasn't until I was very old that I remembered who I was, that I was from the sky. You see, I had shape-shifted into being a human being and was so busy being human I forgot who I really was. I knew it was time for me to go home to the sky again. But there was a problem I couldn't solve. I had forgotten how to shape-shift. I didn't know how to get home or what to do.

Many months later, I had a dream. In this dream my grandfather spoke to me and gave specific instructions to visit your elementary school. He said, "Be there at 1:00 on Tuesday. Your teacher is expecting you. When you wake up you'll find an old suitcase with many things in it. Take it with you to the school."

My grandfather then said, "If a fourth grader asks you how to shape-shift, something special will happen. You will remember how to shape-shift. When you remember, you must then teach them. Only when this is done will you be able to return to the sky."

So thank you my dear fourth graders for helping me return to my family in the sky. I will never forget what it was to be human and I especially will never forget you. And now as your teacher reads the end of my letter, I'm going to prove to you that none of this was just a dream. Everything that has happened here today is true and real.

At that moment the letter began to change its shape into a white circle. The circle twisted and turned, making itself into a cloud, a white cloud that floated to the window. Every boy and girl faced this cloud with open mouths and wide eyes. What they saw never had been written or spoken about before. One by one the cloud turned into the shape of every animal the children knew. At one moment, the cloud looked like a kitten, then a puppy, then a pony, and on and on, until every possible animal shape had been created.

The students by this time were by the window, as close as they could get to this little cloud. With the sound of thunder in the air, the cloud began to swirl into the shape of the old man who had come to their class that day. They were able to clearly see his white hair, long white beard, and worn out white hat. With a smile, the old cloud man winked and went right through the classroom window and floated upward and upwards into the sky. All that could be heard was a far away giggling whisper, "Get ready for Wavy. He is coming to teach you."

As you can imagine, every boy and girl in that class never forgot what took place that Tuesday afternoon. Every one of them now looks at the sky with a strong sense of wonder and mystery.

I'm willing to bet that after hearing this story, you won't be able to look at a cloud or the sky in the same way. That's how powerful shape-shifting can be.

DREAM WORLDS

When I was a young person, I had a repeating dream about floating in a hot air balloon. The balloon kept rising and rising until it hit the edge of the blue sky. The sky's edge was fragile and cracked as if it were a painted egg shell. I went right through the sky and entered a world with colors so unbelievably beautiful that it made the previous world seem unnatural. In this other world there was always a rainbow in the sky.

In these dreams I began learning about the worlds that exist outside everyday reality. These other worlds may be entered when we break through the sky, fall into the earth, or find a secret opening or door in our dreams.

After the third time I had the dream about the crack in the sky, I went to the public library to investigate the nature of dreams. There were all kinds of books on dreams. Most of them tried to explain their hidden meanings. Those books seemed to be guessing without much knowledge of what dreams were really about. I say this because I was able to find a book that revealed everything there is to know about the reality of dreams. It was simply titled, *Dream Worlds* written by Alice Glass.

I checked the book out and took it home with me. That evening after reading a few pages of the book, I fell asleep and met Alice Glass in my dreams. She said it would take three evenings for me to read her book and for her to teach me all I needed to know about dreams. Raising her voice she spoke, "Tonight is your first lesson, so listen carefully and don't forget a thing."

She then jumped into the air and kept going straight up as if there was no gravity to bring her down. "Come on and jump up here," she shouted to me. "You don't need a balloon this time." I wondered how she knew about the balloon that had taken me through the sky. It didn't take long for me to take a big jump and sure enough, up into the sky I went. It was not really flying in the sense we usually think of flying. I felt more like a rocket aimed straight toward the evening sky.

Alice slowed down until she and I were holding hands and travelling upwards together. She confidently turned to me and said, "Brace yourself and prepare for the entry." Within minutes we broke right through the sky as if it were made of the thinnest material on earth.

On the other side of the sky was the dream world I had been to three times before. "Where are we?" I asked Alice. She replied, "Oh, this is only one of many worlds you can visit in your dreams. It has a nice rainbow doesn't it?" Alice then showed me things I had never even thought of in my wildest imagination. She taught me how to fly through mountains and fly through rivers, lakes, and oceans. Everything you could possibly do in the world of the rainbow was taught to me that first evening.

On the second night I read most of the book she had written. As I fell asleep, I heard the voice of Alice. She said to keep my eyes closed because she wanted to introduce me to the world of dream sounds. I learned there are dream worlds where the sounds are so perfect and rich that you become completely absorbed by them. Even if you opened your eyes you wouldn't see anything because all of your attention would be on listening to those remarkable sounds. I was told that the only time this purely takes place on earth is in the midst of a Grateful Dead Concert when the audience-band-audience-band connection becomes a sacred circle of improvisation creating a Mind of Music that breathes sound into everyone present.

In the dream world of sounds, I heard many voices and many sounds I had never heard before. Alice not only taught me to listen to this dream world, she taught me how to make my own sounds. Here you could make any sound you wanted. You could speak as a leopard or whistle like a mocking bird. It was even possible to sound like a guitar, a drum, bass, synthesizer, or a whole music group. Once Alice said, "Listen to this." She then began making the sounds of what she called "The Grateful Dead Orchestra of the Soul."

Alice told me how people believe the famous musical composer, Beethoven had been deaf. I learned how he had actually entered the dream world of sound. Alice also told me about the legendary jazz pianist people refer to as "The Wild Man," a man from the mountains of the Phillipines. He grew up without a piano and no one could figure out how he learned to be such a great pianist. He learned, I found out, by having his own piano inside his head, that is, inside the dream world of sound.

"This is the place where you will learn about the secrets of music and sound," Alice told me as we were returning to the everyday world. "The rainbow world," she went on to say, "is where all enlightened Deadheads learn to enter anything they want to understand. Tomorrow you will learn about *the openings.*"

It was impossible for me to concentrate on anything else that day. What did Alice mean by "the openings?" It was easy for me to understand the world of sound. Once you heard that world, you knew what it meant. All that was necessary in that reality was to make the sounds you wanted to express. Of all the worlds, that one was my favorite. When you've played dream music, you don't want to do anything else.

Years later I discussed this with a professional keyboardist named Keith and he said the whole purpose of being a musician was to be able to enter and hear that world. Playing music had nothing to do with practicing, although some people mistakenly believed it did. Music was a way of trying to unlock the door to the magical world of dream sound. When you enter that world, the music plays right through your whole body without any effort. Every great musician, whether a classical performer or rock star, has had a taste of this experience.

The first dream world, the rainbow world, was almost as amazing as the world of sound. It took me a while to learn that the rainbow world was where I had to go if I wanted to understand something. If I wanted to understand another person, I would go to this world and fly through them. If I wanted to understand what it was like to be an eagle or a bear, I would fly to the rainbow world and fly right through them. When I went through something or someone in this way, it was possible to understand how they feel. This was the knowledge necessary to know what it meant to be in the other person's situation and life.

With great anticipation I waited for the third evening when I would be with Alice for the last time. It was to be the final time she would teach me and as she promised, I would learn about "the openings."

That evening I only had to read the last three pages of the book. To my great surprise there were only three words on those pages, one word per page. These words were pain, suffering, and love. When I fell asleep, Alice came quickly and said, I must now teach you about the three most mysterious things in life. These are *pain, suffering,* and *love.*"

She began her lesson by singing me a song and holding out her hand. When I held her hand she moved me right through her in the same way I had flown through a mountain in the rainbow world. Then she said, "I can only teach you if you understand me. That's why I have brought you into my heart. I must make some music so you will forget all the things that distract your mind."

After the music she explained how no human being can avoid pain and suffering. "Everyone will feel the pain of sickness, injury, loss, grief, tragedy, disappointment, sorrow, fear, shame, embarrassment, hate, jealousy, envy, anger, sadness, frustration, boredom, and failure. You would not be a human being if you didn't feel these pains. Furthermore, we will find that some of the pains will never completely go away. The pains we must learn to live with are called our suffering. When you lose someone you love, you will always carry that pain with you. That is one way we will each suffer."

Alice said that most people don't understand why human beings were made to have pain and suffering. She said, "Everyone tries to run away from these experiences and no one is able to do so. The biggest mystery in the entire universe," she explained, "is understanding that pain and suffering are openings to the dream worlds. On your planet, the custodians of this sacred knowledge are gifted with the talent to play the blues. One of these former carriers of the truth, Pigpen, asked me to bring this wisdom to those you call Deadheads. That's why I have come to you.

"Rather than fight the pain or the suffering, allow it to break the edge of the sky. Allow it to carry you into the other side. Allow it to open your mind, heart, and soul to move you to create the sacred sounds. Without these openings, magic would be absent. It is pain and suffering that help open the doors to the other worlds. Death is the door to life. This is the great secret of all grateful dead."

Alice then said, "I'm going to let you feel my pain and my suffering. When you move through me, allow that pain and suffering to break your heart. Think of that breaking as a breaking of the sky that holds you inside this world. Allow yourself to be broken so you may fly into the other world and understand my suffering. Then carry that feeling and that understanding to the world of sound and allow it to express itself in song. There you will find the most powerful lesson I have to teach. Do this and tell me what you find."

Alice allowed me to feel her pain and suffering. I trusted what she had told me. Rather than fighting the tears and emotions that came through me, I allowed them to open my heart and carry me into a new world of understanding. This, in turn, gave me wings to voice a great song and create a celestial choir and orchestra that gave praise and joy to the wonder of Alice's life.

As I wept over the joy of the music that filled the room, I heard Alice say, "My dear friend, ask yourself what you now feel." I knew what I felt and with all the sincerity and emotion I could gather, I said, "Alice, I feel love."

"Yes," Alice replied, "love is the magic that changes pain and suffering into joy. Never forget what you have learned and know that I am with you always. We are now a part of one another through our understanding of these great mysteries. Be grateful that you will die many times in order to gain entry into life."

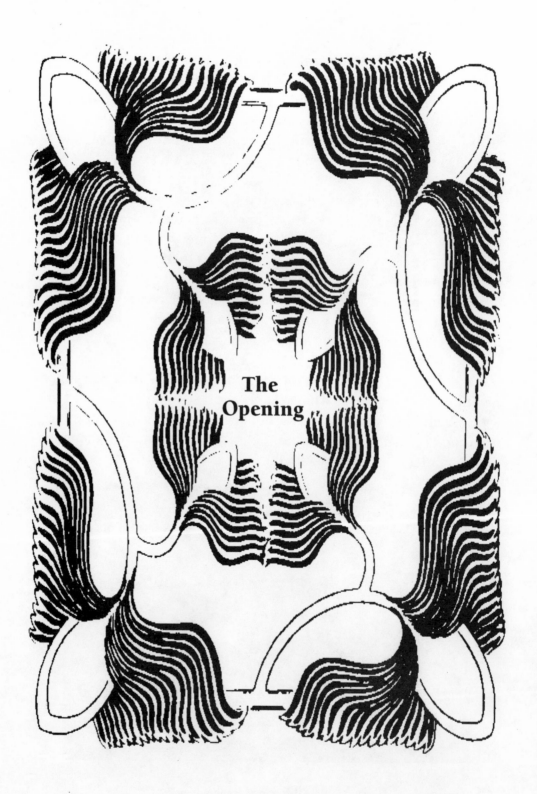

The
Opening